The History of Accounting

This is a volume in the Arno Press collection

The History of Accounting

Advisory Editor
Richard P. Brief

Editorial Board
Gary John Previts
Stephen A. Zeff

*See last pages of this volume
for a complete list of titles*

THE EFFECT OF THE CONCEPT OF THE CORPORATION ON ACCOUNTING

Robert T[homas] [Sprouse]

ARNO PRESS

A New York Times Company

New York — 1976

Editorial Supervision: SHEILA MEHLMAN

———◆———

First publication in book form, 1976
  by Arno Press Inc.'

Copyright © 1956 by Robert T. Sprouse

Reprinted by permission of Robert T. Sprouse

THE HISTORY OF ACCOUNTING
ISBN for complete set: 0-405-07540-5
See last pages of this volume for titles.

Manufactured in the United States of America

———◆———

Library of Congress Cataloging in Publication Data
Sprouse, Robert Thomas.
    The effect of the concept of the corporation on
accounting.

    (The History of accounting)
    Reprint of the author's thesis, University of Minne-
sota.
    Bibliography: p.
    1. Corporations--Accounting. I. Title. II. Series.
HF5686.C7S695   657'.95   75-18486
ISBN 0-405-07568-5

THE EFFECT OF THE CONCEPT OF THE

CORPORATION ON ACCOUNTING

by

Robert T. Sprouse

A Dissertation Submitted to the Graduate Faculty
of the University of Minnesota in Partial
Fulfillment of the Requirements for the
Ph.D. Degree, Major in Business
Administration

August, 1956

TABLE OF CONTENTS

CHAPTER I

INTRODUCTION

The vast majority of commercial enterprise is conducted by means of incorporated business units.[1] It is not
surprising, therefore, that a considerable amount of modern
accounting thought and effort has been focused on the accounting for corporations.

It is the function of financial accounting to provide information of a financial nature which may be used
in the making of decisions. Many of those who supply the
funds with which corporate activities are conducted are
quite removed from participation in the actual control and
direction of affairs of the enterprise. To the corporation
board of directors, presumably elected by the common shareholders, is delegated the responsibility for the establishment of policies and the selection of corporation officers
to administer those policies. This arrangement requires
that periodic reports concerning the results of corporate
operations and the financial condition of the corporation

---

[1]It has recently been reported that although corporations currently represent little more than one-eighth
of the total number of operating businesses, "about three-
fourths of private nonagricultural national income and
employment outside the professions originates in the corporate sector." Betty C. Churchill, "Business Population
by Legal Form of Organization," Survey of Current Business,
XXXV (April, 1955), p. 14.

be made by "management" to those who have invested their
funds and acquired a financial interest in the corporation.

It is reasonable to expect that future decisions to
retain or dispose of such financial interests, usually
evidenced by corporate securities, will be conditioned, at
least in part, by the information contained in financial
reports. Likewise, prospective investors may well be influenced in their decisions to invest or refrain from investing in particular corporations by the financial reports
of those corporations. And, because of the nature of certain unique legal rights with which incorporated business
organizations are endowed and because of the nature of certain
unique legal restrictions which are imposed upon corporations,
information resulting from the financial accounting process
is also used in reaching judicial decisions.

The responsibility of those engaged in financial
accounting is thus clear. The periodic financial statements which represent the culmination of the financial accounting process must be presented in the most reliable and
useful fashion possible within the practical limitations
which exist. Many accountants have expressed the opinion
that the procedures necessary to accomplish this task must,
in certain significant respects, be based on a particular
underlying concept of the corporation. The so-called
proprietary theory of accounting is based on the corporation
conceived as a convenient arrangement for dealing with an
association of individual proprietors. In contrast, the

entity theory of accounting embraces the notion of the
corporation as something which is quite separate and distinct from the individual security holders.[1]

On the grounds that neither the proprietary theory
of accounting nor the entity theory of accounting constitutes a completely satisfactory frame of reference for
financial accounting, a fund theory of accounting has been
proposed in which the corporation is completely "nonper-
sonalized" and the assets of the corporation are looked
upon merely as a "fund" employed in a given set of activities.[2]

It has also been suggested that because both the
structure and behavior of the large corporation are different from that visualized under the proprietary and entity
theories that the large corporation be looked upon as a
social institution rather than as a separate entity or an
association of proprietors. This view is the basis for a
proposed enterprise theory of accounting.[3]

In spite of the apparent importance of the basic concept of the corporation in the formulation of a self-con-
tained accounting theory, there has been, as far as can be

---

[1]The proprietary and entity theories of accounting
are treated in greater detail in chap. iv, infra.

[2]See William J. Vatter, The Fund Theory of Accounting
and Its Implications for Financial Reports (Chicago: The
University of Chicago Press, 1947), and the discussion in
chap. iv, infra.

[3]See Waino W. Suojanen, "Accounting Theory and the
Large Corporation," The Accounting Review, XXIX (July, 1954),
and the discussion in chap. iv, infra.

determined, no comprehensive comparative study of the effects on accounting analysis of the various corporate concepts which are, ostensibly at least, the foundation for proposed theories.[1] Indictments such as the proprietary theory is "seriously defective" as a framework for corporation accounting,[2] or "neither the proprietary theory nor the entity theory is a wholly satisfying frame of reference for accounting,"[3] or the "two traditional frames of reference that are found in accounting theory" are inadequate,[4] have not been supported by demonstrations of the undesirable results of accounting analyses based on the corporate concepts to which objections are made.

Although avowedly a particular concept of the corporation forms the basis for a proposed "theory" of accounting, it is not always clear in what way the proponents' consequent analyses are consistent with the concept advocated and inconsistent with other "theories." Irreconcilable

---

[1]Newlove and Garner have made some comparisons of the proprietary and entity theories but the points compared are largely philosophical rather than analytical, their comparisons are by no means comprehensive, and it is not at all clear why some of the implications they identify with one theory or the other should be so identified. George Hillis Newlove and S. Paul Garner, _Advanced Accounting_, Vol. I (Boston: D. C. Heath and Company, 1951), pp. 20-25.

Vatter has also compared a few of the results of accounting analyses based on the proprietary, entity, and fund theories but there was apparently no concerted attempt to do so and accordingly it is quite incomplete. William J. Vatter, "Corporate Stock Equities," _Handbook of Modern Accounting Theory_, Morton Backer, ed. (New York: Prentice-Hall, Inc., 1955), pp. 359-423.

[2]William Andrew Paton, _Accounting Theory_ (New York: The Ronald Press Company, 1922), p. iii.

[3]Vatter, _op. cit._, p. 7. [4]Suojanen, _op. cit._, p. 391.

conflicts of interpretation, inadequately explained, appear
in the literature.[1] Even within the same publication confusion occurs.[2]

The current status of the various "theories" of accounting which have been proposed as bases for accounting
analysis and reporting suggests an appropriate area of .
investigation. In the accounting for corporations, the
proprietary theory, entity theory, fund theory, and enterprise theory are each held to be based upon an underlying
notion of the corporation. To what extent do differing
concepts of the corporation actually require an accounting
analysis which produces significantly unique results?

Accounting, however, is not an end in itself. If corporate accounting analysis is affected by underlying concepts
of the corporation, to make the accounting product most useful the analysis should not be based on a concept of the

[1]For example, Paton and Paton state that the proprietary approach "underlies, at least implicitly, the
persisting minority view" that "stock dividends" represent income to the recipient stockholders. William A.
Paton and William A. Paton, Jr., Corporation Accounts and
Statements (New York: The Macmillan Company, 1955), p. 2.
In direct contradiction, Husband declares that from the
proprietary point of view "no dividend--cash or stock--
is . . . to be interpreted as income" to the recipient.
George R. Husband, "The Entity Concept in Accounting,"
The Accounting Review, XXIX (October, 1954), p. 557.

[2]For instance, in W. A. Paton and A. C. Littleton,
An Introduction to Corporate Accounting Standards (American
Accounting Association, 1940), it is reasoned that "emphasis
on the entity point of view . . . requires the treatment
of business earnings as the income of the enterprise itself until such time as transfer to the individual participants has been effected by dividend declaration" (p. 8),
yet it is also asserted that the "accumulated balance of
the income account" is an "acknowledged element of stockholders' equity" (p. 105).

corporation invented independently by accountants; rather, it should be based on a concept which is recognized and utilized by those making use of accounting information.

A review of the legal literature and of legal decisions will be undertaken first, therefore, to determine what concepts of the corporation have been recognized as relevant factors in reaching legal decisions. A similar review of the literature of economics will be undertaken to determine what concepts of the corporation have been proposed as being most useful in economic analysis. Then a detailed examination of the concepts of the corporation underlying proposed "theories" of accounting will be made in order to determine the extent to which these "theories" are consistent or inconsistent with the bases for legal and economic analyses. This will be followed by a comparative study of the effect on accounting of those corporate concepts found to be significant in the fields of law and economics. Such a study may be useful in determining whether, in accounting analysis, reliance on various underlying concepts of the corporation produces different results in terms of accounting information. And, if so, such a study may also facilitate the selection of a concept of the corporation which constitutes an acceptable basis for the accounting analysis required to provide useful and valid information for use in making legal and economic decisions.

CHAPTER II

CONCEPTS IN LAW

Introduction

The corporation is frequently referred to as a
"legal entity" and that term is not without significance.
The legal aspect of the process of incorporation is one
of complying with certain specified requirements contained
in the statutes of the state in which incorporation is
desired. Typically, a major requirement is the filing of
articles of incorporation by the incorporators with the
secretary of the state. The articles of incorporation
describe the corporation to be formed--its name, its purpose, its location, a detailed description of the shares
of stock to be authorized, and other prescribed information. If the articles are found to be in conformity with
the statutory requirements, the secretary of the state
of incorporation then issues a "certificate of incorporation" and the corporate existence legally begins. In law,
"legal entity" is defined as legal existence.[1] Clearly,
the corporation has a legal existence upon the issuance

---

[1]Black's Law Dictionary, 4th ed. See also Department of Banking v. Hedges et al., 286 NW 281 (1939).

of the certificate of incorporation.[1]

The significance of the establishment of legal entity
lies in the powers bestowed by the state statutes upon the
duly organized corporation. Among the most important of
these powers are the power to continue as a corporation
for a prescribed length of time or even perpetually; the
power to sue and be sued; the power to acquire, hold, and
convey real and personal property; and the power to enter
into contracts.

In the interests of justice, however, the courts
have found it necessary to look beyond the mere fact of
legal entity and to render decisions conditioned, at least
in part, by underlying concepts of the corporate form of
organization. Thus, discussions and controversies concerning the underlying nature of the corporation have
developed and may be found in abundance in legal literature

---

[1]A corporation which has been duly formed in conformity with the statutes of the state of incorporation is
said to be a de jure corporation. Under certain circumstances, a corporation not so formed may have legal recognition and is said to be a de facto corporation. In
general, a de facto corporation exists where there is a
valid law under which a corporation may be formed, a bona
fide attempt to comply with such law has been made, and
corporate powers have been exercised. For certain purposes, a corporation may also be deemed to exist by estoppel. Estoppel prevents the taking of a position that a
corporation does not exist where previously the position
has been taken that a corporation did exist and where it
would be unjust to allow the denial of corporate existence.

The legal entity of a de jure corporation is clear.
The legal entity of a de facto corporation or corporation
by estoppel is a matter for determination by the courts.

and judicial decisions.

The most popularly advocated concepts are (1) that
the legal entity is an independent existence quite distinct and separate from its officers and stockholders,
and (2) that the legal entity is merely a convenient arrangement for dealing with the association of individuals
actually composing the corporation. A more detailed discussion of these concepts, as found in law, follows.

There are two other concepts found in the legal
literature which also merit consideration. These are the
suggestions that "corporation" merely refers to a set of
legal relations and that the corporation is an economic
institution rather than a legal body.

Association of Individuals Concept

Throughout the long history of corporation law the
view has persisted that corporations are merely associations of individuals united for a common purpose and permitted by law to use a common name. For convenience, the
corporation may be considered a "legal entity" or "legal
person," but this convenient designation is not meant to
obscure the fact that the corporation itself is the
association of individuals interested in it as stockholders.

Corporate acts are the collective acts of the members
of the association; corporate will is the expression of
the collective will. Clearly there could never be complete unanimity of opinion as to every corporate act or

decision; therefore, a provision is made by which the
association may be represented in a practical manner by
representatives empowered to act for the association and
to make its decisions. The common provision that directors
be chosen by majority vote of the stockholders is the
method used for the selection of these representatives.

This concept of the nature of the corporation has
been expressed by many noted scholars in the field of
corporation law. It can best be explained in the words
of those who advocate it. Among the first to record this
view was Kyd, who did so in 1793 in the following fashion:

> A corporation then, or a body politic, or body
> incorporate, is a collection of many individuals,
> united into one body, under a special denomination,
> having perpetual succession under an artificial form,
> and vested, by the policy of the law, with the capac-
> ity of acting, in several respects, as an individual,
> particularly of taking and granting property, of
> contracting obligations, and of suing and being sued,
> of enjoying privileges and immunities in common, and
> of exercising a variety of political rights, more or
> less extensive, according to the design of its insti-
> tution, or the powers conferred upon it, either at
> the time of its creation, or at any subsequent
> period of its existence.[1]

It is to be noted that the core of Kyd's statement
is that "a corporation . . . is a collection of many individuals" and that the remainder of the statement describes
the collection.

About a century later, in 1886, Morawetz subscribed
to this concept by writing:

---

[1] Stewart Kyd, A Treatise on the Law of Corporations
(London: J. Butterworth, Fleet-Street, 1793), p. 13.

A legally constituted corporation is ordinarily treated at law, as well as in the transaction of ordinary business, as a distinct entity or person, without regard to its membership. In most cases this is a just as well as convenient means of working out the rights of the real persons interested; however, it is essential to a clear understanding of many important branches of the law of corporations to bear in mind distinctly, that the existence of a corporation independently of its stockholders is a fiction; and that the rights and duties of an incorporated association are in reality the rights and duties of the persons who compose it, and not of an imaginary being.[1]

. . . .
The statement that a corporation is an artificial person, or entity, apart from its members, is merely a description, in figurative language, of a corporation viewed as a collective body: a corporation is really an association of persons, and no judicial dictum or legislative enactment can alter this fact.[2]

In an article first published in the Columbia Law Review in 1909 and later included in a collection of his essays which was published in 1923, Hohfeld stated:

When all is said and done, a corporation is just an association of natural persons conducting business under legal forms, methods, and procedure that are sui generis. The only conduct of which the state can take notice by its laws must spring from natural persons--it cannot be derived from any abstraction called the "corporate entity." To be sure, the conduct of those individuals will be different when they are cooperating in their collective or corporate projects than when they are acting independently of one another--in a word, the "psychical realities" will be different; but ultimately the responsibility for all conduct and likewise the enjoyment of all benefits must be traced to those who are capable of it, that is, to real or natural persons. When, therefore, in accordance with the customary terminology, we speak of the corporation, as such, as contracting in the corporate name, as acquiring, holding, and transferring property, and as suing

---

[1]Victor Morawetz, A Treatise on the Law of Private Corporations (2d ed.; Boston: Little, Brown, and Company, 1886), I, 3.

[2]Ibid., p. 221.

and being sued, and when we speak of stockholders
as mere claimants against the corporation, holding
stock, which is a species of personal property--
and so on indefinitely--we are merely employing a
short and convenient mode of describing the complex
and peculiar process by which the benefits and
burdens of the corporate members are worked out.[1]

More recently, in 1949, Stevens presented a strong

case for the association of individuals concept and advo-

cated a common basis of analysis for the problem of unin-

corporated as well as incorporated associations.

> The banishment of the medieval conception of a
> corporation as a fictitious nonphysical person and
> the admission that corporate personality is attrib-
> uted to the shareholder would be accompanied by a
> more general recognition that individuals other than
> corporate shareholders have dual legal personalities.[2]
> . . . .
> The more realistic view, that a corporation is
> but a group of individuals associated under legal
> sanction, eliminates the difficulties arising from
> the alleged difference between the physical charac-
> teristics of an individual and the nonphysical
> character of a corporation.[3]

This concept of the corporation as an association

of individuals has likewise been prominent in judicial

decisions. A few illustrations of its application in

practice follow.

In 1874, the Baltimore and Potomac Railroad Company

constructed an engine house and machine shop in Washington,

---

[1]Wesley N. Hohfeld, Fundamental Legal Conceptions
as Applied in Judicial Reasoning and Other Legal Essays,
ed. by Walter Wheeler Cook (New Haven: Yale University
Press, 1923), pp. 198-200.

[2]Robert S. Stevens, Handbook on the Law of Private
Corporations (2d ed.; St. Paul: West Publishing Co.,
1949), p. 45.

[3]Ibid., p. 51.

D. C., within a few feet of the building of the Fifth
Baptist Church, a private corporation. Among other things,
sixteen engine house smokestacks were constructed lower
in height than the windows of the main room of the church.
The noise, smoke, cinders, dust, and offensive odor greatly
annoyed and gradually diminished the congregation, so the
corporation, the Fifth Baptist Church, sued the railroad
for damages. In its charge to the jury, the trial court
stated: "The suit is brought by a congregation duly incorporated and they have brought an action to recover
damages for their inconvenience and discomfort in consequence of the acts of the defendant. It is the personal
discomfort more than anything else which is to be considered in regard to the assessment of damages."[1] The defendant
urged, on the other hand, that the jury be instructed that
"the plaintiff could not recover, being a corporation, for
any inconvenience which members of the congregation assem-
bled in its church might suffer from the noise and offensive
odors occasioned by the defendant's engines and shops."[2]
The trial court refused to give such instructions and
the jury found for the plaintiff. The judgment was ap-
pealed and ultimately affirmed by the United States Supreme
Court in 1883. Associate Justice Stephen J. Field delivered
the opinion which was, in part, as follows:

---

[1]Baltimore and Potomac Railroad Company v. Fifth
Baptist Church, 108 US 323 (1883).

[2]Ibid., pp. 325-326.

The right of the plaintiff to recover for the
annoyance and discomfort to its members in the use
of its property, and the liability of the defendant
to respond in damages for causing them, are not affected by their corporate character. Private corporations are but associations of individuals united
for some common purpose, and permitted by law to
use a common name, and to change its members without
a dissolution of the association. Whatever inter-
feres with the comfortable use of their property,
for the purposes of their formation, is as much the
subject of complaint as though the members were
united by some other than a corporate tie.[1]

In a case decided by the Supreme Court of Ohio in
1900, a stockholder of the Cincinnati Volksblatt Company
requested permission to inspect its books and records.
The request was refused on the grounds that the request
was not in good faith. The stockholder then brought suit
against the corporation. Judge William T. Spear, in re-
citing the opinion in favor of the stockholder, had this
to say:

. . . The rights of the plaintiff in this case are
based upon a recognition of his standing as an integral part of the corporation. The idea that the
corporation is an entity distinct from the corpora-
tors who compose it, has been aptly characterized
as "a nebulous fiction of thought." Much learning
has been indulged in and much space occupied by
text-writers and others in an effort to differen-
tiate the essential character of a corporation
from that of its stockholders, and great ingenuity
has been displayed in the argument, but it has been
in the main a fruitless metaphysical discussion.
For the purpose of description and in defining

[1] Ibid., pp. 329-330. The statement, "Private corporations are but associations of individuals united for
some common purpose, and permitted by law to use a common
name, and to change its members without a dissolution of
the association," was cited in support of a similar United
States Supreme Court decision in a later case, United
States v. Trinidad Coal and Coking Company, 137 US 169
(1890).

corporate rights and obligations, and characterizing
corporate action, the fiction that the corporation
is an artificial person or entity, apart from its
members, may be convenient and possibly useful, but
in the opinion of the writer the argument favoring
the essential separate entity of the corporation
fails, and it is believed that the effort has re-
sulted in misleading conceptions and in much confusion of thought upon the subject. When all has
been said it remains that a corporation is not *in
reality* a person or thing distinct from its constituent parts, and the constituent parts are the stockholders, as much so in essence and in reality as the
several partners are the constituent parts of the
partnership. Stripped of misleading verbiage, the
corporation is a device created by law whereby an
aggregation of persons who may avail themselves of
its privileges by organization, are permitted to
use their property in a way different from that
which is permitted to others who do not so organize,
and with certain special advantages, among which
are a measure as to personal liability for debts,
and the power to perpetuate the organization, denied
by law to all others. With this conception of a
corporation, it would seem to follow as matter of
course, that the property of a corporation, although
subject under some conditions to rights of creditors,
is, in the last analysis, that of the stockholders,
and that when one seeks an inspection of its books,
records, or property, he is in reality but seeking
an inspection of his own, and that this should be
accorded fully, freely, and at all times when such
inspection will not unreasonably inconvenience others
who have like interest in and rights to the property,
and that the attempt to unreasonably hamper such
inspection, by officers. managers, or others, is
an unjust exercise of power and one which courts
should not sanction.[1]

In 1931, the Metropolitan Holding Company, Inc.,
was organized by the directors of the Vandeventer National
Bank to purchase shares of the same Vandeventer National
Bank which were then held by the financially unsound
Vandeventer Securities Company. It was planned that this

----

[1]The Cincinnati Volksblatt Company v. Hoffmeister,
62 Ohio 200-201 (1900).

bank stock would be resold at a profit and the profit
would be paid into the bank to restore its impaired capital.
In 1932, the comptroller of the currency determined that
it was necessary to enforce the statutory "double liability" of the stockholders of the Vandeventer National
Bank and ordered an assessment to the extent of the par
value of its outstanding shares. The Holding Company
failed to pay the assessment on shares still held by it
and proceedings were instituted for the collection of the
assessment from the stockholders of the Holding Company.
In finding the stockholders of the Holding Company liable
the court stated:

> There has been a growing tendency upon the part
> of the courts to disregard corporate entity and to
> treat the stockholders thereof as an association of
> individuals when the interests of justice are to be
> served.[1]

The Metropolitan Holding Company case is rather
typical of a number of cases in which the corporation is
regarded explicitly as an association of persons where
the privilege of corporate legal entity is used "to defeat
public convenience, justify wrong, protect fraud, or defend crime."[2]

---

[1]Metropolitan Holding Company v. Snyder, 79 Fed(2d)
266 (1935).

[2]The words of District Judge Sanborn in United States
v. Milwaukee Refrigerator Transit Co. et al., 142 Fed 255
(1905).

Concept of Separate and Distinct Entity

Clearly, the corporation concept most frequently
expressed in judicial decisions is that the corporation
is a legal entity separate and distinct from the corporation officers and stockholders. It cannot be said with
equal confidence, however, that this is the predominant
view among authors of treatises on corporation law or
writers of articles appearing in legal periodicals. And,
among those who regard the corporation as a separate and
distinct entity, there is considerable disagreement as to
whether the entity is created by the state or merely recognized by the state and whether the entity is a fiction or
is a reality. Because the courts are usually silent as
to these finer points the practical legal significance of
these differences is not easy to assess. Such distinctions
are, however, the basis of a vast amount of discussion in
articles and books dealing with corporation law.

Basically, there are three separate theories of the
separate and distinct legal entity: the "fiction theory,"
the "concession theory," and the "realistic theory." The
essence of the so-called fiction theory is that when a
corporation is formed an artificial or fictitious person
or personality is created which is separate and distinct
at law from the natural persons whose interests it embraces.

A closely related theory emphasizes that a corporation cannot arise out of a mere agreement between the

members but can exist only as a creature of the state,
the result of the gift of the franchise by the state.
The franchise being in the nature of a concession from
the sovereign, this has been referred to as the "concession
theory" or "sovereign theory."

A third group agree that the corporate entity is
separate and distinct from the corporation stockholders
and officers and further insist that it is not artificial
but natural, not fictitious but real. It is maintained
that the corporation has a will of its own and a volition
identifiable from the individual volitions of the stockholders. It is believed that the real entity comes into
existence when the group comes into existence, and it does
not depend upon the state to create it even though its
legal status must necessarily depend upon recognition by
the state.

The theory of the fictitious legal person apparently
originated with Pope Innocent IV in the thirteenth century.
The doctrine was stated as the reason why corporate bodies
or _universitas_ could not be punished or excommunicated--
they had neither a soul nor a body and had being only _in_
abstracto.[1] A leading proponent of this view was the
German law scholar, Savigny, writing in the early nineteenth century and adopting this theory based on his study

---

[1]John Dewey, _Philosophy and Civilization_ (New York:
Minton, Balch and Company, 1931), pp. 152-159.

of early Roman law.[1] He reasoned that the essential attri-
bute of a natural subject of rights and duties involves
the possession of a will and yet, in law, property belongs
to the corporation and not to any individual. Inasmuch
as a corporation does not really possess a will, it must,
as a property-owner, be a fictitious person.

> The law authorizes the corporation to act in many
> other respects as though it were a natural person,
> which of course it is not, except in the intendment
> of the law. To this extent, namely, that the law
> treats the corporation as a person for many purposes,
> the element of fiction is therefore involved in the
> corporate conception.[2]

This fictitious person is separate and distinct from
the shareholders because it may own property in its own
name, it may prosecute and defend by legal action in its
own name, the debts and assets of the corporation are not
the debts and assets of the shareholders, it may contract
with a shareholder as though there were no connection
between it and such shareholder, and it may survive the
death or changing membership of any or all of its shareholders.

The concession theory, while often confused with
the fiction theory, had a different origin. It is essentially a product of the rise of the national state at a

[1]For a complete philosophical discussion of the
Savigny theory see Frederick Hallis, Corporate Personality:
A Study in Jurisprudence (London: Oxford University
Press, 1930), Pt. I, chap. i.

[2]I. Maurice Wormser, Frankenstein, Incorporated
(New York: McGraw-Hill Book Company, Inc., 1931), p. 63.

time when religious congregations and guilds were rivals
of the claim of the national state to complete sovereignty.
The restricting of capacity to act as a corporation only
to those bodies having positive authorization represented
a check on the tendency of group action to undermine the
liberty of the individual by unfair practices or to rival
the political power of the state.[1]

According to Dewey,

> It is clear that there is nothing essentially in
> common between the fiction and concession theories,
> although they both aimed toward the same general con-
> sequence, that of limitation of the power of corporate
> bodies. The fiction theory is ultimately a philo-
> sophical theory that the corporate body is but a
> name, a thing of the intellect; the concession theory
> may be different as to the question of the reality
> of a corporate body; what it must insist upon is
> that its legal power is derived.[2]

The concession theory is exemplified in Kent's

Commentaries on American Law:

> A corporation is a franchise possessed by one or
> more individuals, who subsist, as a body politic,
> under a special denomination, and are vested, by the
> policy of the law, with the capacity of perpetual
> succession, and of acting in several respects, how-
> ever numerous the association may be, as a single
> individual.[3]
> . . . .
> A corporation being a mere political institution,
> it has no other capacities or powers than those which
> are necessary to carry into effect the purposes for
> which it was established.[4]

---

[1]Dewey, op. cit., pp. 152-159, and Stevens, op.
cit., pp. 6-8.

[2]Dewey, op. cit., p. 157.

[3]James Kent, Commentaries on American Law (14th ed.;
Boston: Little, Brown, and Company, 1896), II, 409.

[4]Ibid., p. 430.

In summarizing the differences between corporations
and partnerships, joint stock companies and business trusts,
Wormser says:

> If there is one element more than any other which
> stands out glaringly it is that the underlying charac-
> teristic of all corporations is the corporate "franchise"
> granted by the sovereign. It is this franchise which
> confers artificial legal personality, immunity from
> individual liability and responsibility on the part
> of the stockholders, and continuous, even perpetual,
> succession. The franchise which grants these valuable
> privileges and immunities necessarily involves the
> assumption of corollary duties and obligations to the
> sovereign. The legal vassal created by the sovereign
> owes obligations of fealty and utmost good faith to
> its creator.[1]

The concession theory has also been expounded in
judicial decisions. For example, in a United States Supreme
Court case, on the grounds that the corporation might be
incriminated, an individual who was an officer of a corporation refused to produce documentary evidence, consist-
ing of correspondence, records, and accounts of the corporation, which had been subpoenaed by a grand jury. Associate
Justice Henry Billings Brown delivered the opinion of the
court:

> . . . The corporation is a creature of the State.
> It is presumed to be incorporated for the benefit of
> the public. It receives certain special privileges
> and franchises, and holds them subject to the laws
> of the State and the limitations of its charter.
> Its powers are limited by law. It can make no con-
> tract not authorized by its charter. Its rights to
> act as a corporation are only preserved to it so
> long as it obeys the laws of its creation. There
> is a reserved right in the legislature to investi-
> gate its contracts and find out whether it has ex-
> ceeded its powers. It would be a strange anomally

---

[1]Wormser, op. cit., pp. 76-77.

to hold that a state, having chartered a corporation
to make use of certain franchises, could not in the
exercise of its sovereignty inquire how these franchises have been employed, and whether they had
been abused, and demand the production of the corporate books and papers for that purpose.[1]

Although there is "nothing essentially in common"
there is likewise no inherent conflict between the concession
theory and the fiction theory. In American law, the statement of Chief Justice Marshall in the case of the Trustees
of Dartmouth College v. Woodward, which was decided in
1819 and which is still widely held as an acceptable statement of the nature of the corporation, contains elements
of each of these theories.

> A corporation is an artificial being, invisible,
> intangible, and existing only in contemplation of
> law. Being the mere creature of law, it possesses
> only those properties which the charter of its cre-
> ation confers upon it, either expressly, or as in-
> cidental to its very existence. These are such as
> are supposed best calculated to effect the object
> for which it was created. Among the most important
> are immortality, and, if the expression may be allowed,
> individuality; properties, by which a perpetual suc-
> cession of many persons are considered as the same,
> and may act as a single individual. They enable a
> corporation to manage its own affairs, and to hold
> property without the perplexing intricacies, the
> hazardous and endless necessity, of perpetual con-
> veyances for the purpose of transmitting it from
> hand to hand. It is chiefly for the purposes of
> clothing bodies of men, in succession, with these
> qualities and capacities, that corporations were
> invented, and are in use. By these means, a per-
> petual succession of individuals are capable of
> acting for the promotion of the particular object,
> like one immortal being.[2]

---

[1]Hale v. Henkel, 201 US 74-75 (1906).

[2]The Trustees of Dartmouth College v. Woodward,
4 Wheaton 636 (1819).

Marshall's statement, however, is in many ways but
an iteration and amplification of the statement of Sir
Edward Coke made some two hundred years earlier in the
English courts in The Case of Sutton's Hospital:

> And it is great reason that an hospital, etc.
> in expectancy or intendment, or nomination, should
> be sufficient to support the name of an incorpora-
> tion when the corporation itself is only in abstracto,
> and rests only in intendment and consideration of
> the law; for a corporation aggregate of many is
> invisible, immortal, and rests only in intendment
> and consideration of the law.[1]

Perhaps the writings of Blackstone also influenced
the thinking and language of Marshall. In 1775, Blackstone
wrote:

> . . . As all personal rights die with the person;
> and, as the necessary forms of investing a series of
> individuals, one after another, with the same iden-
> tical rights, would be very inconvenient, if not
> impracticable; it has been found necessary, when
> it is for the advantage of the publick to have any
> particular rights kept on foot and continued, to
> constitute artificial persons who may maintain a
> perpetual succession, and enjoy a kind of legal
> immortality.
>   These artificial persons are called bodies
> politic, bodies corporate, (corpora corporata) or
> corporations.[2]

The fiction theory and concession theory may very
well be viewed as being complementary: the corporate person is fictitious because it was created artificially by
the state.

----

[1]The Case of Sutton's Hospital, 10 Coke 32.

[2]William Blackstone, Commentaries on the Laws of
England (7th ed.; Oxford: Clarendon Press, 1775), I, 467.
(Italics mine.)

Among the most prominent to challenge the fictitious
nature of the separate and distinct entity and its creation
by the state was another German scholar of the law, Otto
von Gierke.[1] Writing near the end of the nineteenth century, he insisted that the natural individual represents
only one type of personality, that he is not the sole pos-
sessor of such volition, acting capacity, and inherent
unity as is held essential to the conception of a "person."
His theory has been summarized as follows:

> Above the existence of the individual there is
> the existence of the species, and the corporation is
> nothing but the legal expression of this fact, which
> appears as a reality in all other spheres of life.
> As the individual will is embodied in the physical
> person, so the higher will of the species is embodied
> in numerous and various forms of association, and as
> a result we find, beside the individual, entities of
> a higher order endowed with volition and acting
> capacity. And where the law recognizes such embodied
> will as a person, we have a juristic person or a cor-
> poration. The law does not create the corporate per-
> son, but finding it in existence invests it with a
> certain legal capacity. The corporation rests upon
> a substratum of physical persons, but it is not
> identical with them, for out of the association of
> the individuals the new personality arises, having a
> distinctive sphere of existence and will of its own.
> If corporate rights are distinguished from individual
> rights it is because they are controlled by this dis-
> tinctive will. The corporation as a person distinct
> from its members is not a fiction, but a reality.[2]

Maitland's translation of Gierke's works was published
in England in 1900. In his Introduction, Maitland condensed
the theory as follows: The corporation in German law was

---

[1]For a complete philosophical discussion of Gierke's
theory, see Hallis, op. cit., Pt. III, chap. i.

[2]Ernst Freund, The Legal Nature of Corporations
(Chicago: The University of Chicago Press, 1897),
pp. 13-14.

"no fiction, no symbol, no piece of the State's machinery,
no collective name for individuals, but a living organism
and a real person, with body and members and a will of its
own. Itself can will, itself can act; it wills and acts
by the men who are its organs as a man wills and acts by
brain, mouth, and hand. It is not a fictitious person;
. . . it is a group-person, and its will is a group-will."[1]
The term "organic theory" has since been applied to indicate
this concept.

A number of English and American writers have supported the reality doctrine[2] and the courts have found some
occasion to express it. An example of judicial application
is a 1943 case before the Supreme Court of Minnesota. The
Minnesota Tribune Company published the Minneapolis Morning
Tribune and other newspapers. In 1941, this company transferred all of its assets to the Star-Journal Company,
another newspaper publishing firm, and the actual printing

---

[1]Frederic William Maitland in his Introduction to
Otto Friedrich von Gierke, Political Theories of the
Middle Age, trans. Frederic William Maitland (Cambridge:
University Press, 1900), p. xxvi.

[2]In addition to Maitland, see W. Jethro Brown, "The
Personality of the Corporation and the State," The Law
Quarterly Review, XXI (October, 1905), 365-379; W. M.
Geldart, "Legal Personality," The Law Quarterly Review,
XXVII (January, 1911), 90-108; Harold J. Laski, "The
Personality of Associations," Harvard Law Review, XXIX
(February, 1916), 404-426; Arthur W. Machen, Jr.,
"Corporate Personality," Harvard Law Review, XXIV (February,
1911), 253-267, and XXIV (March, 1911), 347-365; Frederick
Pollock, "Has the Common Law Received the Fiction Theory
of Corporations?" The Law Quarterly Review, XXVII (April,
1911), 219-235.

of the Minneapolis Morning Tribune was transferred to the
Star-Journal building. Two Minnesota Tribune Company
employees, whose employments were transferred to the Star-
Journal Company without any loss of work, brought suit
against the Minnesota Tribune Company for severance pay
on the grounds that the sale of its newspaper assets constituted a dismissal. The defendant Minneapolis Tribune
Company continued in existence as the holder of one-third
of the stock of the Star-Journal Company and claimed severance had not been effected.

The court, in deciding in favor of the plaintiffs,
the two employees, said:

> Defendant's position becomes untenable when we
> consider that it and the new Star-Journal and Tribune
> Company are distinct and separate entities. The
> nature of a corporation is such that it is an entity
> separate and distinct from the body of its stock-
> holders. . . . It is not a fiction of the law but
> a real legal unit possessing individuality and en-
> dowed by the law with many of the attributes of
> persons. . . . The transfer of interest was as com-
> plete and effective as it would have been if the
> Tribune Company had received no stock in the Star-
> Journal Company.[1]

These three theories--the fiction theory, the concession theory, and the reality theory--have been considered
together because they are in agreement as to the separate
and distinct nature of the legal entity. As indicated
earlier, there is much discussion in the literature based
on the differences between these three theories. It is
felt by some, however, that whether the legal entity is

---

[1]Matthews et al. v. Minnesota Tribune Co., 10 NW(2d)
232 (1943).

fictitious or real, or is created by the state or merely
recognized by the state, is relatively insignificant. As
Wormser says,

> Practical minds generally have refused to enter
> into any discussion of whether the incorporeal person
> is a fiction or a reality. They regard this as just
> as foolish as discussing whether a jackass located
> midway between two bundles of hay will turn to one
> or the other, or as profitless as the medieval dis-
> cussion of how many angels could dance on the point
> of a needle.[1]

And John Chipman Gray, noted Harvard University
Professor of Law, said:

> Whether a corporation is a fictitious entity, or
> whether it is a real entity with no real will, or
> whether, according to Gierke's theory, it is a real
> entity with a real will, seems to be a matter of no
> practical importance or interest. On each theory
> the duties imposed by the state are the same and
> the persons on whose actual wills those duties are
> enforced are the same.[2]

In support of this view, shared by Wormser and Gray,
it may be noted that the judicial decisions from which the
preceding citations were excerpted were probably not dependent upon the real or fictitious nature of the corporation.[3] The notion of separate and distinct corporate
entity, however, is a concept of considerable practical
importance. This may be demonstrated without further
consideration of the fiction, concession, or reality which

---

[1] Wormser, op. cit., p. 60.

[2] John Chipman Gray, The Nature and Sources of the
Law (2d ed.; New York: The Macmillan Company, 1927), p. 55.

[3] Cf. The Trustees of Dartmouth College v. Woodward,
p. 22, supra; The Case of Sutton's Hospital, p. 23, supra;
and Matthews et al. v. Minnesota Tribune Co., p. 26, supra.

might be involved. There are a large number of judicial
decisions in which this concept has been expressly adopted.
Only three of these are noted here as samples of the extreme circumstances in which this concept of the corporation
has been upheld.

In the state of Virginia some land, the deed to which
contained a covenant to the effect that the title to the
land was never to be vested in a Negro or Negroes, was purchased by a corporation whose capital stock was held ex-
clusively by Negroes. The purchase was for the express
purpose of converting the property into an amusement park
for Negroes. An individual brought suit to have the covenant
enforced and the conveyance to the corporation canceled.
The Virginia Supreme Court of Appeals, in 1908, in holding
in favor of the corporation, cited Cook's concept: "A
corporation is an artificial person, like the state. It
is a distinct existence--an existence separate from that
of its stockholders and directors."[1] Marshall's concept
was likewise cited[2] and the court found that because "a
corporation is a person which exists in contemplation of
law only, and not physically" the sale of the land to the
corporation was not a sale to a Negro or Negroes.[3]

---

[1] William J. Cook, A Treatise on the Law of Corporations Having a Capital Stock (8th ed.; New York:
Baker, Voorhis & Co., 1923), I, 2.

[2] See p. 22, supra.

[3] People's Pleasure Park Co., Inc. et al. v. Rohleder,
61 SE 794 (1908).

A case not unlike the Virginia case arose in England
after the outbreak of the First World War. A company which
was incorporated in England but the capital stock of which
was held, all but one share, by German subjects residing
in Germany and the directors of which were also German
residents and citizens, sued to enforce payment of a debt.
The defendant admitted the debt but resisted payment on
the grounds that inasmuch as it was unlawful to have commercial intercourse with alien enemies, payment to the
corporation was illegal. Lord Reading, speaking for the
court, said:

> It cannot be disputed that the plaintiff company
> is an entity created by statute. It is a company
> incorporated under the Companies Acts and therefore
> is a thing brought into existence by virtue of statu-
> tory enactment. At the outbreak of the war it was
> carrying on business in the United Kingdom; it had
> contracted to supply goods; it delivered them, and
> until the outbreak of the war it was admittedly en-
> titled to receive payment at the due dates. Has the
> character of the company changed because on the out-
> break of war all shareholders and directors resided
> in an enemy country and therefore became alien enemies?
> Admittedly it was an English company before the war.
> An English company cannot by reason of those facts
> cease to be an English company. It remains an
> English company regardless of the residence of its
> shareholders or directors either before or after the
> declaration of war. Indeed it was not argued . . .
> that the company ceased to be an entity created under
> English law, but it was argued that the law in time
> of war and in reference to trading with the enemy
> should sweep aside this "technicality" as the entity
> was described and should treat the company not as an
> English company but as a German company and therefore
> as an alien enemy. . . . The fallacy of the appellants'
> contention lies in the suggestion that the entity
> created by statute is or can be treated during the
> war as a mere form or technicality by reason of the
> enemy character of its shareholders and directors.
> A company formed and registered under the Companies
> Acts has a real existence with rights and liabilities

as a separate legal entity. It is a different person altogether from the subscribers to the memorandum
or the shareholders on the register. . . . Once it is
validly constituted as an English company it is an
artificial creation of the Legislature and it retains
its existence for all intents and purposes. It is a
living thing with a separate existence which cannot
be swept aside as a technicality. It is not a mere
name or mark or cloak or device to conceal the identity
of persons. . . . It is a legal body clothed with the
form prescribed by the Legislature.

In determining whether a company is an English or
foreign corporation no inquiry is made into the share
register for the purpose of ascertaining whether the
members of the company are English or foreign. For
the appellants' contention to succeed payment to the
company must be treated as payment to the shareholders
of the company, but a debt due to a company is not a
debt due to all or any of its shareholders. . . . The
company and the company alone is the creditor entitled
to enforce payment of the debt and empowered to give
to the debtor a good and valid discharge. Once this
conclusion is reached it follows that payment to the
plaintiff company is no payment to the alien enemy
shareholders or for their benefit.[1]

Even more recently, in 1933, the following circumstances were brought before the Supreme Court of Massachusetts:
A contract between a corporation and a labor union provided
that the corporation should employ union members only. Some
time later, because it was thought the union was allowing
other employers to pay lower wages, a new corporation was
organized to carry on the business as an open shop, free
of the obligations under the union contract. The same
officers and shareholders held the same offices and number
of shares in the new corporation as they had held in the
old. The first corporation sold its property to the second
corporation; the first corporation relinquished its lease

[1]Continental Tyre and Rubber Co., Ltd. v. Daimler Co.,
1 KB 903-904 (1915).

and the second corporation took a new lease on the same
premises; the first corporation discharged its employees
and the second corporation employed a force of nonunion
men. The union sued the two corporations to enjoin viola-
tion of their contract but the court held in favor of the
corporations, saying:

> The motive of the officers, directors and stock-
> holders of the old corporation, as individuals, that
> is, the desire of these incorporators of the new cor-
> poration to secure through the instrumentality of a
> corporation authority to do business exactly like
> the business done by the old corporation without the
> burden of the commercial agreement as to the employ-
> ment of union labor, cannot be regarded as fraudulent
> in fact or in law. Corporations, like individual
> stockholders, are distinct entities; neither can be
> treated as agents of the other when openly contract-
> ing for themselves and in their own names. . . . "In
> the absence of a fraudulent purpose in the organiza-
> tion of a corporation, it is settled law in this
> Commonwealth that the ownership of all the stock and
> the absolute control of the affairs of a corporation
> do not make that corporation and that individual
> owner identical. Nor do such ownership and control
> make the property of the corporation subject to the
> payment of the stockholders' debts," nor subject
> the corporation to liability upon contracts which
> it has neither executed nor assumed.[1]

The Corporation as a Set of Legal Relations

The legal literature of the past thirty years reveals
attempts by some writers to establish a concept of the corporation more in keeping with modern developments. In
particular there is evident discontent arising from attempts
of the courts to maintain the sanctity of the separate and
distinct corporate entity only to find that the corporate

---

[1]Berry v. Old South Engraving Co., 186 NE 604-605
(1933).

entity must be disregarded if justice is to prevail.
Terms such as "piercing the corporate veil" and "disregard
of the corporate entity" have become commonplace in judicial decisions and legal literature. It must be mentioned also, however, that some writers have argued that
the separate and distinct nature of the corporate entity
should be upheld and that disregard by the courts has been
unnecessary.[1]

At least two new concepts have emerged, or are
emerging, as these modern developments in corporation law
take place. Some writers and judges suggest that it is
futile to attempt to personify the corporation--to look
upon the corporation as some kind of legal person or entity.
Whether it be real or fictitious, "corporation" should be
accepted merely as a convenient term indicating a given
set of legal relations. Whether it is a "corporation sole,"
a "corporation aggregate," an "association of individuals,"
or a "separate and distinct legal entity" is not relevant--
the act of incorporation endows the business enterprise
with certain immunities and privileges prescribed by
statute and common law.

A second group of writers advocate the recognition
of the "economic entity" rather than the "legal entity."
The economic entity theory has been discussed and illustrated

---

[1]See George F. Canfield, "The Scope and Limits of
the Corporate Entity Theory," Columbia Law Review, XVII
(February, 1917), 128-143; and George S. H. Sharratt, Jr.,
"Corporations--Nature and Theory--Why Corporate Entity?"
Missouri Law Review, I (June, 1936), 278-281.

particularly in connection with problems arising from the
parent-subsidiary relationship of a group of two or more
affiliated corporations. It has been suggested that such
a group of corporations be recognized as a single economic
enterprise and dealt with, in law, as a single economic
entity rather than as separate and distinct legal entities.
But the theory is deemed applicable in many other branches
of corporation law as well.

Perhaps the clearest expression of the view of the
corporation as merely a set of legal relations is that of
Judge Nathan Bijur of the New York State Supreme Court in
1927 in the case of Farmers' Loan and Trust Co. v. Pierson
et al. The nature of the corporation was very much in
issue in this case. The trustees of an estate, consist-
ing solely of all the outstanding shares of a corporation,
elected themselves directors of that corporation and then,
refusing to account to the beneficiaries of the estate
for their management of the corporation, restricted their
accounting for the estate to only the continuing custody
of the stock and the receipt of dividends. The beneficiaries urged that they were entitled to know from the
trustees, to a reasonable extent, all facts concerning the
management of the corporation which was being conducted by
the trustees under their title as directors. The trustees,
on the other hand, offered the existence of the corporation
as their reason for declining to follow the ordinary course
of trustees, namely, the giving of a full account of their
substantial acts.

In his decision, Judge Bijur reviewed the concepts
referred to earlier in this paper as fiction theory, concession theory, and reality theory, and the association of
individuals concept and concluded:

> My conclusion from the foregoing review is that
> the law has neither a "personality" nor an "entity"
> to deal with, and that there is no "veil." These terms
> are useful as metaphors or figures of speech to meet
> a common need in discussing the legal principles in-
> volved. . . .
> . . . A corporation is more nearly a method than
> a thing, and . . . the law in dealing with a corpora-
> tion has no need of defining it as a person or an
> entity, or even as an embodiment of functions, rights
> and duties, but may treat it as a name for a useful
> and unusual collection of jural relations, each one
> of which must in every instance be ascertained, ana-
> lyzed and assigned to its appropriate place according
> to the circumstances of the particular case, having
> due regard to the purposes to be achieved. A confirma-
> tion of the accuracy of this analysis of the corpora-
> tion form is found in the fact that the word "coporation"
> has a variable, not a constant, meaning.
> The rights and obligations that are comprised
> within the compass of the word change not only with
> time, but with locality. Limited liability of the
> shareholders is a comparatively recent invention.
> Limited and unlimited liability existed side by side,
> even within this state, under the Laws of 1875. The
> extent of limited liability varies under different
> statutes. Corporations with no par stock are now
> quite common. Methods of transacting business, con-
> ditions under which dividends may be declared, and
> all the details of what are commonly known as corporate
> activity are actually different in different jurisdic-
> tions. Moreover, endless variants of those features
> may be conceived of without doing violence to the
> general designation "corporation."[1]

The central theme of this statement was given favor-
able recognition a few years later by Surrogate Wingate
when in discussing concepts of the corporation he said,
"Perhaps the best of all is the statement of Mr. Justice

---

[1]Farmers' Loan and Trust Co. v. Pierson et al.,
222 NYS 543-544 (1927).

Bijur that it /corporation/ is merely a name for a useful
and usual collection of jural relations."[1]

After his survey of the historical background of the
"corporate legal personality," John Dewey concluded:

> As far as the historical survey implies a plea for
> anything, it is a plea for disengaging specific issues
> and disputes from entanglement with any concept of per-
> sonality which is other than a restatement that such
> and such rights and duties, benefits and burdens, accrue
> and are to be maintained and distributed in such and
> such ways, and in such and such situations.[2]

Taylor also conceives of the corporation as a set of
legal relations:

> . . . A corporation is to be regarded as a legal insti-
> tution. In this sense it means the sum of legal rela-
> tions existing in respect to the corporate enterprise.
> Let us analyze the term "legal institution." It de-
> notes a body of legal rules in their manifestations
> in legal relations between persons as to whom certain
> mutually related conditions of fact may be affirmed.[3]
> . . . .
> . . . A corporation, considered as a legal institu-
> tion, is the sum of the legal relations resulting from
> the operation of rules of law in its constitution
> upon the various persons, who by fulfilling the pre-
> requisite conditions, bring themselves within the
> operation of these rules.[4]

Another writer, advocating that less significance be
placed upon prevailing corporate concepts, expressed the
opinion that "the defects of the intransigent conceptualism
which apparently accompanies the entity technique is of

---

[1]In re Steinberg's Estate 274 NYS 919 (1934).

[2]Dewey, op. cit., p. 159.

[3]Henry O. Taylor, A Treatise on the Law of Private
Corporations (5th ed.; New York: The Banks Law Publishing
Co., 1905), pp. 18-19.

[4]Ibid., p. 25.

itself a source of danger in legal thinking."[1] The theme
of his discussion was that decisions should not be based
on either the existence or disregard of the corporate entity but rather on the facts of the case.

> A corporation, then, like any composite whole,
> may present different aspects for different purposes.
> For some purposes the attention is directed to the
> entity as an organized collectivity, and, while the
> identity of the individual stockholders is not denied,
> it is really immaterial to the purposes at hand. There
> is no fatal objection to framing this thought some-
> what differently, by familiarly saying that the entity
> is separate and distinct, other than the danger that
> in a later situation too much significance be credited
> to the statement in that form. For other purposes
> the identity of the individual stockholders becomes
> important just as do for some purposes the component
> parts of a house or a ship, and then one does not say
> that the corporation is an entity separate and dis-
> tinct from its stockholders.[2]

He characterized the corporate entity as "but a name by
which a complex can be dealt with in discourse, a simple
device of securing limited liability and facilitating
reference to a complicated group of relations."[3]

Concept of Economic Entity

The central notion of the concept of economic entity
is the substitution of economic realities for prevailing
juridical concepts. As modern business has developed,
increasing use has been made of the corporate device as
a "nonconductor" between the stockholder and the business

---

[1]Elvin R. Latty, Subsidiaries and Affiliated Corporations (Chicago: The Foundation Press, Inc., 1936), p. 27.

[2]Ibid., pp. 15-16.

[3]Ibid., p. 15.

enterprise. It has become increasingly more difficult
for the courts to adhere to the widely accepted concept
of the corporation as a separate and distinct entity. In
order to mete justice the courts have found it necessary
to disregard the corporate entity and examine reality.
In the words of Berle, "The corporation is emerging as an
enterprise bounded by economics, rather than as an artificial mystic personality bounded by forms of words in a
charter, minute books, and books of account. The change
seems to be for the better."[1]

The recognition of the economic entity by the courts
is well illustrated by a recent case. The Pittsburgh
Railways System was created, in 1902, without its own corporate charter, by means of leases and operating agreements
with a large number of corporations, referred to as "underliers." The properties were operated by the Pittsburgh
Railways Company in conjunction with its own. In 1938,
the Company filed a petition for reorganization under the
Bankruptcy Act. No proceedings were filed by or against
any of the underliers so, in order to maintain a unified
system of transportation for Pittsburgh and surrounding
municipalities, the City of Pittsburgh petitioned the
District Court to exercise jurisdiction over the underlier
corporations. Some of the underliers moved to dismiss the
petition but the petition was granted by the Court of
Appeals. In his opinion, Judge Herbert F. Goodrich said:

[1]Adolph A. Berle, Jr., "The Theory of Enterprise
Entity," Columbia Law Review, XLVII (April, 1947), 345.

As we see the question, the issue is whether the demand of the facts is to control or whether obeisance must be made to the doctrine of the separate corporate entities of all these concerns which, from the business point of view, constitute one operation and one enterprise. . . .[1]

. . . . Our conclusion is that the facts of the present case call for the treatment of this great transportation system as one entity for purposes of reorganization, regardless of the elaborate jig-saw puzzle arrangement of all the underlying companies which have gone into it. In so concluding we emphasize the nearly half century of physical operation of this enterprise as a unit, with the interchange of movable property, routes, operating personnel and everything involved on the business side. We recognize the necessity of the unitary economic foundation for it. . . . We are concerned with the realities of the situation. . . .We think that the many years of factual unity and the public necessity for the measures which will insure the proper economic foundation for the system, override the arguments for the recognition of the legal concept of separate entity on the part of the underliers.[2]

Another case has been cited as an example of the courts' recognition of the economic entity where one individual owns substantially all the stock of a corporation.[3] In Wood v. Guarantee Trust and Safe Deposit Company, Starr owned all but five hundred shares of the stock of the City of Joliet Water Works Company. Using money which ought to have been applied to the payment of materials used in construction of the water works, Starr acquired some past-due coupons from holders of the Water Works Company bonds. These coupons were, in turn, transferred to Wood in payment

---

[1]In re Pittsburgh Railways Company, 155 Fed (2d), 482 (1946).

[2]Ibid., p. 485.

[3]Maurice J. Dix, "The Economic Entity," Fordham Law Review, XXII (December, 1953), 264.

of the construction materials. When Wood presented the
coupons, payment was refused on the grounds that the
coupons were effectively "extinguished, canceled, and
paid" when Starr purchased them. Associate Justice Lamar
of the United States Supreme Court delivered the opinion
of the court which was unfavorable to Wood and from which
the following remarks have been excerpted:

> Starr is essentially (that is, from a business
> point of view) the Water Works Company, owning as he
> does, 19,500 of its 20,000 shares of stock. Its
> prosperity is manifestly his prosperity, its disaster
> his disaster, and any disbursement made by it is sub-
> stantially made by him.[1]
> . . . .
> The same consideration of the substantial identity
> between Starr and the Water Works Company is of great
> weight in the determination of the remaining question.[2]
> . . . .
> The case before us is a peculiar one, and must be
> adjudged on its own facts. As we have already said,
> Starr was, from a business point of view, substan-
> tially the company. Not only was it his object to
> float the bonds, but to float the company, as well.[3]

The court looked upon Starr, an individual, and the
Water Works Company, a corporation, not as two distinct
legal entities, which for some purposes would have been
quite proper, but rather looked upon the individual and
the corporation as a single legal unit. The interests of
the Water Works Company and Starr were so intermingled
and inseparable as to constitute one economic entity. It
is to be noted that a court which viewed the corporation

---

[1] Wood v. Guarantee Trust and Safe Deposit Company,
123 US 424 (1888).

[2] Ibid., pp. 424-425.

[3] Ibid., p. 425.

as an association of individuals might have dealt with this
case in precisely the same fashion. However, these two
concepts, economic entity and association of individuals,
call for identical analysis only where the corporation
is very closely held and controlled. Advocates of the economic entity would not consider the more than one million
stockholders of the American Telephone and Telegraph Company
and that corporation to comprise a single economic entity.

Analysis of these and other cases of a similar nature
have prompted some to urge explicit recognition of the economic nature of the business enterprise rather than its
legal form.

> In its financial power and in its unified direction
> and control, the corporation plays a significant role
> in modern economic life. It is thus absurd to consider
> the corporation as an individual. If the corporation
> is to be personified at all, it appears that it should
> be personified as an economic unit. It may be even
> termed an "economic" person.[1]

And

> A legal entity differs from an economic entity.
> The economic entity does not have any corporate charter.
> It is an economic choice of management. It ties in
> legal entities for operation in a common endeavor or
> enterprise. The idea behind an economic entity is
> joinder or merger of activity--unity of life--in the
> goal of the common undertaking or enterprise. In an
> economic entity, each legal entity has dedicated it-
> self and its property to the success of the common
> undertaking.[2]
> . . . .
> Combined or coordinated operations--in whole or
> in part--of the business or activities of a group of

[1]Joseph Wise, "Due Process: Corporation as an
Economic Unit," University of Cincinnati Law Review, XIII
(May, 1939), 467.

[2]Dix, op. cit., p. 255.

corporations, clearly results in a unity of life in
the common endeavor. It is an economic arrangement
of activity defining the function to be performed by
each participant in the enterprise. It rests on the
facts of economic life and not on the form of separate
legal entity. It carries out the intended economic
arrangement of the enterprise. Those who deal with
the economic entity as such should not be required to
examine the details of the legal structure.[1]

As an indication of the increasing significance of
the concept of economic entity, remarks of other well-known
authors in the field of corporation law and finance may be
noted. Berle calls attention to the fact that "the divergence between corporate theory and the underlying economic
facts has occasioned a variety of problems (dealt with
ad hoc by the courts) in which the theory of 'artificial
personality' simply did not work, and was consequently extended, disregarded, sometimes buttressed by further fiction, at others manipulated to get a convenient result."[2]
He suggests that a number of rules, ordinarily regarded
as separate, are, in fact, applications of a single dominant principle. It is his contention "that the entity
commonly known as 'corporate entity' takes its being from
the reality of the underlying enterprise, formed or in
formation; that the state's approval of the corporate form
sets up a prima facie case that the assets, liabilities,
and operations of the corporation are those of the enterprise; but that where the corporate entity is defective,
or otherwise challenged, its existence, extent, and

_____

[1] Ibid., p. 264.

[2] Berle, op. cit., p. 344.

consequences may be determined by the actual existence and
and extent and operations of the underlying enterprise,
which by these very qualities acquires an entity of its
own, recognized by law."[1] Berle refers to this as the
"enterprise entity," whereas we have referred to it as
the "economic entity."

Dewing also considers the "true conception" of the
corporation to be one which emphasizes its economic nature
rather than its legal nature:

> The legal attributes of the corporation are mere
> accidents of historical development; they do not de-
> scribe the corporation as we understand it, nor do
> they give us any clue to its social and economic sig-
> nificance in our modern industrial society. . . . The
> corporation is an institution and its reality lies
> not in legalistic definitions but in the part the
> corporation plays in the complex balance of forces
> that constitutes the economic world of the present
> time. What we are interested in, if we try to define
> a corporation, is its functions, as an institution--
> and a very important and significant institution--in
> our contemporary economic life.[2]

Means, an economist, collaborated with Berle in a
study of the "modern" corporation and their conclusions
were published in The Modern Corporation and Private
Property. As a result of this study they advocated a
"new concept of the corporation"--one which recognizes
the corporation's increased economic and social status.
The dominant finding leading to this concept was the

---

[1]Ibid., p. 344.

[2]Arthur Stone Dewing, The Financial Policy of
Corporations (5th ed.; New York: The Ronald Press
Company, 1953), I, 16-17.

significant separation of ownership and control in the modern corporation.[1]

According to Berle and Means, the "traditional logic of property" requires that the stockholders be recognized as the owners of the corporation and, therefore, requires that the stockholders receive the profits of industry. The management group in control of the corporation occupy a position of trusteeship and are obliged to operate the corporation for the sole benefit of the security holders.

The "traditional logic of profits" requires that "if profits must be distributed either to the owners or to the control, only a fair return to capital should be distributed to the 'owners'; while the remainder should go to the control as an inducement to the most efficient ultimate management."[2]

Because neither of these alternatives is acceptable nor convincing, Berle and Means advocate recognition of the corporation as a social institution.

[1]Among the statistics presented to indicate the extent of the separation of ownership and control were the results of a 1925 study of the Federal Trade Commission. The directors and officers of 4,367 corporations, selected in a manner to give a cross-section of all industry, were found to own on the average only 10.7 per cent of the common and 5.8 per cent of the preferred stocks of the corporations with which they were associated. The study indicated further that as the size of the company increases, the tendency to dispersion increases. Adolf A. Berle, Jr., and Gardiner C. Means, The Modern Corporation and Private Property (New York: The Macmillan Company, 1936), pp. 50-52.

[2]Ibid., p. 344.

Neither the claims of ownership nor those of control can stand against the paramount interests of the community. . . . It is conceivable,--indeed it seems almost essential if the corporate system is to survive,--that the "control" of the great corporations should develop into a purely neutral technocracy, balancing a variety of claims by various groups in the community and assigning to each a portion of the income stream on the basis of public policy rather than private cupidity.[1]

Summary

An evaluation of the validity and usefulness of the preceding four concepts of the corporation will be postponed until an examination of concepts in economics has been accomplished. At this point, however, the incompatibility of the association of individuals concept, the concept of separate and distinct legal entity, and the notion of economic entity is evident. The corporation cannot be both separate and distinct from the stockholders and also merely a convenient name for the stockholders themselves. A group of affiliated corporations cannot constitute a single significant economic entity if they are quite separate and distinct from one another. And the economic interests of the holders of widely distributed shares of a corporation's securities are clearly not intermingled with the economic operations of that corporation to such an extent as to constitute a single unified economic entity. Finally, if "corporation" is purely a term for a set of legal relations it can have no more conceptual significance in economics and accounting than other legal terms such as "agency" and "bailment."

---

[1]Ibid., p. 356.

CHAPTER III

CONCEPTS IN ECONOMICS

Introduction

In general, economists have not found it necessary
to develop any unique theory to deal with corporations.
Rather, it has been traditional to utilize the concept of
the "firm" as a unit for analysis and, for the most part,
the legal form of the "firm" has not been relevant.

The firm has been defined variously as "the unit
within which productive resources are combined to turn out
goods and services for sale"[1] and "a complex of productive
resources--persons and things yielding useful services--
where services are directed under a common plan and authority to the maximization of profit for the owners of the
enterprise."[2] The "firm" may be further understood by
indicating its usual relation to "plant" and "industry."
A "plant" is usually a physical unit of production, con-
sisting of land, buildings, and other physical equipment,
owned by a firm; the "firm" is a business unit under unified

---

[1]Mary Jean Bowman and George Leland Bach, Economic
Analysis and Public Policy (2d ed.; New York: Prentice-
Hall, Inc., 1950), p. 49.

[2]Albert G. Hart, "Anticipations, Planning and the
Business Cycle," Quarterly Journal of Economics, LI
(February, 1937), 277.

46

ownership and control, which in turn may own and operate
one or more plants; and an "industry" consists of all the
firms engaged in the production of a given commodity.[1]
Any particular firm, then, may belong to several industries
and be comprised of any number of corporate entities. It
is not uncommon for a firm to incorporate its various divisions separately, perhaps creating an administrative corporation, a manufacturing corporation, a selling corporation,
etc., or to incorporate individual plants separately, particularly where different commodities are produced.

The corporation, then, is usually looked upon as
essentially a legal rather than a strictly economic concept.
Whether the "firm" is a sole proprietorship, a partnership,
or a corporation is of no consequence in much of economic
analysis. This is not to say that the development of the
modern corporation has not created any problems for economic theory. In particular, there has been difficulty
and controversy in applying the concept of entrepreneurship
and economic profits to the corporate form of business organization. There is considerable difference of opinion
as to the economic relationship of the shareholder and the
corporation. It is in this regard that the attitudes and
analyses of economists become relevant to this study.

Prevalent views concerning the identification of
entrepreneurship in the modern corporation with widely
distributed securities may be grouped into three categories.

[1]Bowman and Bach, op. cit., pp. 49-50.

There are those economists who consider the common shareholders to be "corporate entrepreneurs"; those who believe
the board of directors, or management, or even that the
corporation itself, as a firm, carries on the entrepreneurial function; and those who consider it futile to
attempt to associate any entrepreneurial function with the
modern corporation. The divergence of views is partially
due to lack of uniformity in the definition of entrepreneurship but largely due to differences in the underlying
concepts of the economic functions of shareholders and
corporate officers.

Common Shareholders as Corporate Entrepreneurs

Prominent among those identifying entrepreneurship
with the common shareholder is Ben W. Lewis. According
to Lewis, "an accurate (and useful) definition of the entrepreneurial function will limit that function to (1) the
taking of responsibility of enterprise, i.e., _willing_ that
enterprise shall go on; (2) such making of ultimate, final
decisions as cannot be delegated, i.e., the making of
decisions inseparably connected with original investment
in enterprise in anticipation of a contingent, residual
return; and (3) bearing of the peculiar uncertainties--
necessary to the institution, and inevitable in the case
of business enterprise--which derive from the fact that
no other functional agent has promised the entrepreneur
to repay his investment or to pay him any return thereon."

Lewis holds that this definition of entrepreneurship can be applied "completely and usefully irrespective of the form of business organization involved, and . . . the corporation, far from exploding and dividing the concept of entrepreneurship, serves really to clarify and to make more distinct its exact nature."[1]

Application to the corporation of this notion of the entrepreneurial function—responsibility taking, uncertainty bearing, and the making of ultimate decisions—is made by Lewis in the following manner.

As to the responsibility of enterprise and risk-bearing, "labor may stand ready to be hired—'directive' or 'executive' as well as manual or routine—and capital may await a borrower; but no production will be undertaken for an uncertain market (however great or small the uncertainty may be) until some agent indicates his willingness to <u>promise</u> payment to the other functional agents and/or to risk the uncertainties of the market, with no promise for his own remuneration from any other functional agent."[2]

Lewis notes that the capitalist and laborer receive from the entrepreneur not <u>guarantees</u> but <u>promises</u>.

It is quite true, of course, that others besides the entrepreneur are forced to bear the burden of uncertainties, but the uncertainties borne by the entrepreneur are peculiar <u>in kind</u>; the laborer may lose his position and fail even to receive wages which he has earned, and the capitalist may lose his capital and his interest; but in both cases payment of the

---

[1] Ben W. Lewis, "The Corporate Entrepreneur," <u>The Quarterly Journal of Economics</u>, LI (May, 1937), 536.

[2] <u>Ibid.</u>, p. 539.

functional incomes, and in the second case the return
of the property as well, are promised by the entrepreneur.
The entrepreneur alone proceeds without the promise of
functional remuneration by any other functional agent.
The uncertainties which he bears are peculiar; they
must be borne by some functional agent if productive
enterprise is to to /sic/ undertaken for an uncertain
market.[1]

The ultimate decisions which cannot be delegated are
attributed to the entrepreneur as one who chooses positively
or by acquiescence--even by indifference--"the persons who
shall make the active decisions relating to the current
conduct of the enterprise, or the persons who shall choose
the persons (many steps may be involved) to make such active
decisions."[2]

> . . . The entrepreneur is located in those persons
> whose functional income is contingent and residual in
> the sense that no claim for income arises until all
> other functional claims are discharged, and particu-
> larly in that no absolute promise for its payment
> is made by any other functional agent. Typically,
> thus, the corporate entrepreneur will be located in
> the common stockholder.

This view is shared substantially by Charles A.
Tuttle. Tuttle's analysis proceeds along different lines,
but his conclusions are much the same.

> In the corporation, already the predominant form
> of the business unit, the body of stockholders with
> voting rights--a juridical person--performs the func-
> tion of the entrepreneur. Though the right to organize

---

[1]Ibid., p. 539. According to Lewis the corporate
stockholder is no less an entrepreneur because he enjoys
limited liability: "The extent of his possible loss is
limited, but the nature of the uncertainty he bears is
no different from that borne by any single proprietor."
Ibid., p. 542.

[2]Ibid., p. 530.

[3]Ibid., pp. 537-538.

and direct the incorporated business unit belongs as
a property right to the shareholders of this type as
a body, its immediate exercise by them is naturally
impracticable. Accordingly, by virtue of the power
which the entrepreneur function gives them, they
choose and hire a "captain of industry" with his staff
of technicians to take immediate command of the enterprise and to organize and direct "the industrial army."
They give him as his share of the product a stipu-
lated wage, determined by the law of wages. The
management of the incorporated business is, therefore, representative management, and is responsible
to those who perform the entrepreneurial function.[1]

According to Tuttle, the distinctive function of the

entrepreneur is "ownership of the business," viewed as an

organized unit. It involves no labor, no capital-owning,

and no ownership of land or other durable production goods.

The personal income which attaches to this function is

economic profit.[2]

Tuttle's concept of entrepreneurship is very closely

related to that of John Bates Clark, who, along with Alfred

Marshall, has been credited as being foremost of recent

economists to stress the "unique importance of this func-

tion."[3] Clark carefully distinguished profits from the

wages of any kind of labor and the interest on any kind

of capital.[4]

---

[1]Charles A. Tuttle, "The Function of the Entrepreneur,"
The American Economic Review, XVII (March, 1927), 24.

[2]Ibid., pp. 13-25. See also Charles A. Tuttle, "The
Entrepreneur Function in Economic Literature," The Journal
of Political Economy, XXXV (August, 1927), 501-521; and
Charles A. Tuttle, "A Functional Theory of Economic Profit,"
Economic Essays in Honor of John Bates Clark, ed. Jacob H.
Hollander (New York: The Macmillan Company, 1927), pp. 321-336.

[3]Maurice Dobb, "Entrepreneur," Encyclopaedia of the
Social Sciences, V (1931), 558.

[4]Clark extends "the traditional theory of rent" so
as to merge the rent of land with "interest."

According to Clark,

> The holders of common stock are always entrepreneurs, and they are also capitalists if the stock represents any real capital actually paid in. If the bonds and preferred stock represent all the real capital that there is, any dividends that may be paid on common stock are a pure entrepreneur's profit. If, on the other hand, the stock all represents money actually put into the business, the dividends on it contain an element of net profit if they exceed simple interest on the capital and insurance against the risks that are not guarded against by actual insurance policies.[1]

Under the term "labor" Clark includes all effort expended in a routine way in carrying on business. "The overseers in the shops, the bookkeepers, clerks, secretaries, treasurers, agents, and, in short, all who perform any of the labor of management for which they get or can get salaries are laborers in the comprehensive sense." He recognizes that, as corporations have become increasingly important, salaried managers have moved more and more into controlling positions. For their efforts, however, they receive "wages." The entrepreneur performs "a special coordinating function which is not labor, in the technical sense, and scarcely involves any continuous personal activity at all, but is essential for rendering labor and capital productive." This latter function is kept distinct from the work of the superintendent or manager of a business.[2]

Clark writes:

> . . . It is important in the bookkeeping of a company to ascertain how much of the return to the

---

[1]John Bates Clark, Essentials of Economic Theory (New York: The Macmillan Company, 1918), p. 122.

[2]Ibid., p. 83.

stockholders is merely interest on the capital they
have themselves invested and how much is true profit,
or the net gain which is over and above interest. In
business life a distinction is pretty clearly maintained between the three kinds of income. . .; namely,
the reward of labor in all its forms, the reward of
capital, going to whoever furnishes it, and the reward of a coordinating function, or the function of
hiring both labor and capital and getting whatever
their joint product is worth above the cost of the
elements which enter into it.[1]

From Clark's point of view, the increasingly significant role of hired managers and the increasingly passive
role of the stockholders merely tend to reduce profits and
detract from "the advantages which the incorporation of a
business offers."[2] One might well infer from this view
that if an entrepreneurial function of "coordination" exists
in the modern corporation and it is performed by the common
stockholders, it consists largely of "hiring" the capital
paid for their own shares and "hiring" a board of directors.
This is essentially Tuttle's view, also. The suggested
tendency toward reduced entrepreneurial or "true" profit
accompanying greater control by salaried managers would
therefore be justified by the reduced significance of the
entrepreneurial function of the shareholder and the grow-
ing tendency for the function of the shareholder to become
largely that of capitalist.

---

[1]Ibid., p. 85. Risk-bearing is apparently not one
of the elements involved in Clark's concept of entrepreneurial activity. He suggests, as indicated earlier, that
"interest" includes "simple interest on the capital and
insurance against risks that are not guarded against by
actual insurance policies." P. 51, supra.

[2]Ibid., p. 89.

Corporate Officials As Corporate Entrepreneurs

The German economist, Herbert von Beckerath, insists that stockholders can no longer be identified with the entrepreneur. He characterizes the entrepreneur of the modern corporation as the "responsible head of the business."

> He is not necessarily the person supplying the capital for the enterprise. It is well to draw a distinction between the entrepreneur as the actual commercial and administrative head of the business, the capitalist (who bears the financial risk of the enterprise and partakes in its changing profits in the form of a dividend), and the mere creditor.[1]

He further suggests that the entrepreneurial function may be shared by several individuals. "One may be the technical, another the financial, and a third the commercial manager."[2] This is to be found particularly in "modern large-scale enterprise." And it is the limitations of the human capacities of the entrepreneur or entrepreneurs which restrict the optimum size of the enterprise.

R. A. Gordon, who has been particularly interested in the management of the large modern corporation, is in agreement with the views of Beckerath.

> It is clear that the great body of passive stockholders, the chief recipients of ownership income, have little to do with active control, and that we must look elsewhere for the true entrepreneur. It is the present writer's opinion--but proof must await more detailed analysis--that much of the entrepreneurial

---

[1] Herbert von Beckerath, _Modern Industrial Organization_ (New York: McGraw-Hill Book Company, Inc., 1933), p. 44.

[2] _Ibid._, p. 45.

function in the 107 companies here studied is exercised by one or at most a few important executives.[1]

Gordon urges a reexamination of "orthodox economic theories" of enterprise and profits in light of modern developments. He believes that any useful concept of the entrepreneurial function must encompass "active decision making and responsibility for policy which is involved in control over allocation of the factors of production and in the direction of the productive process."[2] Income to passive owners is not entrepreneurial income and may be to some extent functionless in nature.

Whereas Gordon stresses "control" as a necessary element of entrepreneurship, Kaldor emphasizes "co-ordination." Kaldor looks upon "co-ordinating ability" as the fixed factor which determines the "technically optimum size" of the firm and accordingly defines the firm as a "productive combination possessing a given unit of co-ordinating ability."[3] He reasons that the task of coordinating the allocation of resources among various investment alternatives and the adjustment of the productive factors to continuously changing economic data may be vested in a

---

[1]Robert A. Gordon, "Stockholdings of Officers and Directors in American Industrial Corporations," The Quarterly Journal of Economics, L (August, 1936), 654.

[2]Ibid., p. 653.

[3]"Coordination" is also the term Clark uses (p. 52, supra), but Kaldor gives it a somewhat different connotation and does not visualize the common shareholder as performing the coordinating function. Nicholas Kaldor, "The Equilibrium of the Firm," The Economic Journal, XLIV (March, 1934), 69.

single individual or, as in the case of the modern corporation, a group of individuals such as a board of directors.
In any event, the shareholder, as such, is not the corporate entrepreneur.

The divergence of the economists' views presented
thus far centers upon the function of the entrepreneur.
Lewis, Tuttle, and Clark are in agreement that the common
shareholders are the corporate entrepreneurs. They agree
that this is so largely because the choice of the board of
directors--whether by positive action or acquiescence--is
an important element in the entrepreneurial function. In
addition, Tuttle considers the common shareholders to be
the "owners" of the corporation who delegate their property
rights to "representative management," and Lewis attaches
importance to the unsecured nature of the common shareholder's investment.

Von Beckerath, Gordon, and Kaldor, on the other hand,
look upon the common shareholder, as such, as solely a
capitalist. The corporate entrepreneur is the individual
or group actively directing the administration of the
business.

Frank Knight takes a position which to some degree
combines the foregoing opposing views. His concept of the
entrepreneur encompasses two fundamental responsibilities:
the assumption of risk and the assumption of management.

> The essence of enterprise is the specialization
> of the function of responsible direction of economic
> life, the neglected feature of which is the insepara-
> bility of these two elements, responsibility and

> control. . . . Any degree of effective exercise of judgment, or making decisions, is in a free society coupled with a corresponding degree of uncertainty-bearing, of taking the responsibility for those decisions.[1]
>
> . . . .
> There is an apparent separation of the functions of making decisions and taking the "risk" of error in decisions. The separation appears quite sharp in the case of the hired manager, as in a corporation, where the man who makes decisions receives a fixed salary, taking no "risk," and those who take the risk and receive the profits--the stockholders--make no decisions, exercise no control.[2]
>
> . . . .
> The apparent separation between control and risk taken turns out . . . to be illusory. The paradox of the hired manager, which has caused endless confusion in the analysis of profit, arises from the failure to recognize the fundamental fact that in organized society the crucial decision is the selection of men to make decisions, that any other sort of decision-making or exercise of judgment is automatically reduced to a routine function.[3]

Knight reasons that in theory the corporation is a representative democracy, of an indirect type. The shareholders elect the directors whose main function, in turn, is to select officers to actually carry on the business of the company. Ordinarily, however, the directors themselves determine general corporation policies. "Moreover if it is a large enterprise, the executive officials chosen by the directors have only a general oversight over business policy, and their chief function in turn is to select subordinates who make most of the actual decisions involved in the control of the concern."[4] Of course, the process does not

---

[1]Frank H. Knight, Risk, Uncertainty, and Profit (Boston: Houghton Mifflin Company, 1921), p. 271.

[2]Ibid., p. 293.   [3]Ibid., 297.

[4]Ibid., p. 291.

stop there; there may be many levels of the hierarchy where
the chief duties are the selection of subordinates. Thus
ultimate "control"[1] is vested in the shareholder having
voting rights. The situs of the ultimate financial responsibility for such control in the shareholder (to the extent
of legal limitations) is not generally questioned.

This view has been belittled by Schumpeter.

> It is extremely interesting to observe that for a
> long time and occasionally even now economic theorists
> have been and are inclined to locate entrepreneurial
> function in a corporation with the shareholders. How-
> ever little the individual small shareholder may have
> to do with the actual management or else with the
> entrepreneurial function in the corporation, they hold
> that ultimate decision still lies with them to be
> exerted in the shareholders' meeting. All I wish to
> say about this is first, that the whole idea of risk-
> taking in this way takes on further lease of life and,
> second, that such a theory is about as true as is the
> political theory that in a democracy the electorate
> ultimately decides what is to be done.[2]

Other Concepts of Corporate Entrepreneurship

Schumpeter's own conception of the entrepreneur is
one which stresses innovation. He considers it "difficult
or even impossible to name an individual that acts as 'the
entrepreneur' in a concern. The leading people in particular, those who carry the titles of president or chairman of

---

[1]According to Knight, "control" consists mainly of
selecting someone else to do the "controlling."

[2]Joseph A. Schumpeter, "Economic Theory and Entre-
preneurial History," Essays of J. A. Schumpeter, ed. by
Richard V. Clemence (Cambridge: Addison-Wesley Press,
Inc., 1951), p. 256.

58

the board, may be mere coordinators or even figure-
heads; . . ."[1] Combining factors into production or planning or designing production is recognized as a distinct
economic function but may be essentially a matter of routine
administration where "combinations that have been carried
into effect in the past had to be simply repeated or even
if they had to be repeated subject to those adaptations
which common business experience suggests in the face of
conditions that change under the influence of external
factors."[2]

The Schumpeter entrepreneur is one who responds crea-
tively to given conditions and acts outside of the realm of
routine. Clearly this concept does not embrace the common
shareholder, as such. The entrepreneurial function must
then be performed within the corporate organization and
in the large-scale corporation that function may be carried
on cooperatively. "Aptitudes that no single individual
combines can thus be built into a corporate personality."[3]
This concept dictates that the function of the shareholder
be solely that of capitalist.

A more extreme point of view concerning the identification of the entrepreneurial function is that taken by
James H. Stauss, who advanced the proposition that the

[1] Ibid., p. 256. Note that Schumpeter refers to "mere
coordinators" whereas Kaldor considers "coordination" the
essential element in entrepreneurship. (Cf. p. 54, supra.)

[2] Ibid., pp. 252-253.

[3] Ibid., p. 256.

<u>firm</u> is the <u>entrepreneur.</u>

. . . with respect to the proposition that the firm
is the entrepreneur, it must be set forth at the beginning that the entity known . . . as <u>the firm</u> is
taken as a real institution. As such <u>the firm exists</u>
apart from the individuals who compose its <u>decision-
making</u> organization, but it <u>does not function</u> apart
from them. Thus the entity <u>is not a fiction;</u> it is
a fact.[1]

Stauss, like Knight, stresses the inseparability of
the managerial decision-making and the active risk-taking
in a meaningful concept of entrepreneurship.

It is clear that risk-bearing must be merged with
risk-taking /decision-making/, because the state of
exposure to a specified loss is fundamentally conditioned by decision-making in the firm. In turn, the
firm, through its decision-making organization as an
aggregate, whatever the groups of which that aggregate is composed, undertakes this active risk-taking,
and the firm as a functional entity is the antecedent
risk-bearer, because it possesses assets and receives
income. Thus, a unique, integrating agency itself
provides a frame of reference for a comprehensive
analysis of enterprise and of the relations of the
various functionaries to the organization of production.[2]

Diametrically opposed to the Stauss concept and representing the other extreme is the position of Charles O.
Hardy, who emphasizes "the impossibility of applying the
concept 'entrepreneur' to any part of a corporate organization (except in a close corporation which is managed like
a partnership). The essence of entrepreneurship is the
union of control and risk-bearing; in a publicly owned

---

[1]James H. Stauss, "The Entrepreneur: The Firm,"
<u>The Journal of Political Economy</u>, LII (June, 1944), 112.
Stauss' concept of entrepreneurship has much in common
with the reality theory of separate and distinct entity.
(Cf. p. 24, <u>supra</u>.)

[2]<u>Ibid.</u>, p. 124.

corporation these are not united."[1]

Summary

In many cases writers in economic theory have obviated the problem of identification of entrepreneurship in the modern corporation by framing their discussions of the entrepreneur and profit in a world of sole proprietorships. As might be expected, this brief review of the divergent views of some of those economists who have implicitly, and sometimes explicitly, expressed themselves concerning the relationship of the shareholders and the corporation does not lead to any compelling conclusion.

Nevertheless, certain consistencies and inconsistencies with the concepts of the corporation found in law may be noted. Clearly, identification of the entrepreneurial function with the common stockholder is compatible with the legal conception of the corporation as an association of individuals. It would be expected that economists who consider the common shareholder to be the corporate entrepreneur would consider the corporation to be an association of entrepreneurs having "a common purpose" and using "a common name."

It would likewise be consistent, in many cases, for those economists who identify entrepreneurship with the board of directors, corporation officers, or the corporation itself, and who consider the passive shareholder to be

---

[1] Charles O. Hardy, *Risk and Risk-Bearing* (Revised ed.; Chicago: The University of Chicago Press, 1931), p. 54.

merely a capitalist, to advocate the legal concept of separate and distinct corporate entity. And to view the firm itself as the entrepreneur, as Stauss does, lends support to the reality theory of the separate and distinct legal entity.

In the case of a parent-subsidiary relationship of a group of affiliated corporations, economic analysis would undoubtedly call for obliteration of the separate and distinct legal entities and the recognition of the "firm" and the board of directors and/or officers controlling the "firm." The "economic entity" advocated by some individuals in law is comparable with this concept of the "firm" in economics.

The problem, created by a group of affiliated corporations, could also be resolved by tracing the "individuals" ostensibly associated in a subsidiary corporation ultimately to the stockholders of the parent corporation. The concept of the corporation as an association of individuals, or entrepreneurs, however, would be acceptable only to those economists who identify entrepreneurship with the common shareholder. Such economists are by no means an overwhelming majority.

Finally, a corporation as a set of legal relations is of no interest in economics. It would perhaps be satisfactory from the viewpoint of Hardy, who suggests there is no entrepreneurial function in the modern, publicly-held corporation. But, in general, such a concept only serves to justify the attitude, referred to earlier, that the

corporation is essentially a legal concept rather than
an economic concept.

CHAPTER IV

CONCEPTS IN ACCOUNTING

Introduction

The two major legal concepts of the corporation have
their counterparts in accounting theory as clearly as they
do in economic theory of the entrepreneur. As was indicated in the introduction to this study, proponents of the
proprietary theory of accounting view the corporation as
an association of individual proprietors. Essentially,
stockholders, partners, and sole proprietors are all placed
in the same category--that of the "owners" of the business.
Presumably, the concept of the corporation inherent to the
entity theory of accounting is identical with the legal concept of separate and distinct entity. In fact, it has been
said that the "entity theory stems from the legal fiction
of the corporate enterprise as a person in its own right."[1]

Moreover, the fund theory of accounting would seem
to be consistent with the legal view of the "corporation"
as merely a term for a particular set of legal relations.
And the concept of the corporation underlying the enterprise
theory of accounting is closely related to what has been
referred to as the legal concept of economic entity.

---

[1]Vatter, "Corporate Stock Equities," op. cit.,
p. 365.

The general implications attributed to each of these
four accounting theories and their rationalization will be
reviewed at this time in order that the succeeding examination of effects on the accounting analysis of specific
transactions might be limited to those underlying corporate
concepts which merit a more detailed consideration.

Proprietary Theory of Accounting

The proprietary theory is evident, explicitly as
well as implicitly, in the writings of many writers in the
field of accounting. One leading proponent of the proprietary theory, George R. Husband, has described the corporation as follows: "For purposes of economics and
accounting, the corporation might well be viewed as a
group of individuals associated for the purpose of business enterprise, so organized that its affairs are conducted
through representatives."[1] The basic accounting implica-
tion derived from this theory is that the stockholders,
through the corporate medium, own all the corporation assets
and owe all the corporation liabilities and that the excess
of assets over liabilities, therefore, represents the
interest or the "proprietorship" of the stockholders.
Accordingly, it has even been suggested that liabilities
be looked upon as negative assets.[2]

---

[1] George R. Husband, "The Corporate-Entity Fiction and
Accounting Theory," The Accounting Review, XIII (September,
1938), p. 242.

[2] See Charles E. Sprague, The Philosophy of Accounts
(New York: The Ronald Press Company, 1922), p. 49, and
A. C. Littleton, Accounting Evolution to 1900 (New York:
American Institute Publishing Co., Inc., 1933), p. 192.

It is recognized, of course, that certain privileges
are granted to the owners of corporate assets that are not
granted to the owners of the assets of a sole proprietorship or partnership. Among the most important of these
privileges are legal limitation of liability for the in-
debtedness of the corporation to the amount of the owners'
investment and the ability to transfer ownership interests
without interfering with the continuity of corporate
activities.

The following comments of Husband pertain to these
unique privileges granted corporate "owners."

> Regardless of the characteristics which the law
> gives to the corporate form of organization, it remains
> an organization of individuals. Basically, it is the
> common stockholders who constitute the entrepreneurs
> in the case of the corporation and who use it for the
> purpose of obtaining profit. The final decisions are
> theirs; they bear the ultimate risk. The characteris-
> tics given to the corporation by the law are designed
> to make more attractive the prospect of earning profit.
> To this end the law endeavors to reduce the nuisance
> value of the activity, and to facilitate the making
> of decisions. From the economic point of view, never-
> theless, the corporation remains an agency organiza-
> tion. Accounting comes closest to reality and to
> being of economic service when it recognizes this fact,
> when it measures "entrepreneurial" success or failure,
> and when it imputes profit or loss to the "entrepre-
> neurial" actors. In so doing it is most consistent
> with the requirements of free enterprise society.[1]

As other concepts of the corporation found in the
accounting literature are examined it becomes increasingly
clear that one of the significant features of the proprietary
theory is the distinction made between creditors and stockholders or liabilities and proprietorship. This distinction

---

[1]Husband, "The Entity Concept in Accounting," op.
cit., p. 558.

is exemplified by one of the important early proponents
of the proprietary theory, Charles E. Sprague, who, writing
in 1907, reasoned as follows:

> The assets being regarded as composed of rights
> against others and the liabilities as others' rights
> against us, the excess of rights in our favor is the
> proprietorship.
> Thus, the right-hand side of the balance sheet is
> entirely composed of claims against or rights over the
> left-hand side. "Is it not then true," it will be
> asked, "that the right-hand side is entirely composed
> of liabilities?" The answer to this is that the rights
> of others, or the liabilities, differ materially from
> the rights of the proprietor, in the following respects:
> 1. The rights of the proprietor involve dominion
>   over the assets and power to use them as he
>   pleases even to alienating them, while the
>   creditor cannot interfere with him or them
>   except in extraordinary circumstances.
> 2. The right of the creditor is limited to a
>   definite sum which does not shrink when the
>   assets shrink, while that of the proprietor
>   is of an elastic value.
> 3. Losses, expenses, and shrinkage fall upon the
>   proprietor alone, and profits, revenue, and
>   increase of value benefit him alone, not his
>   creditors.
> For these reasons the proprietary interest cannot
> be treated like the liabilities and the two branches
> of the right-hand side of the balance sheet require
> distinctive treatment.[1]

The proprietary view is also advocated by Moonitz
and Staehling. To them "corporateness is essentially a
device which makes it possible for a few or a great multi-
plicity of proprietors (stockholders) to join in a common
enterprise with a magnitude of investment far beyond the
amount which any one of them could possibly muster or

---

[1]Sprague, op. cit., pp. 52-53. That Sprague's remarks were intended to be applicable to the corporation
is evident from illustrations containing Capital Stock
and Surplus accounts and from subsequent comments.

might wish to contribute."[1] They look upon the recognition of the corporation as a legal entity endowed with the ability to act in law as a natural person might act, the provision for transferability of corporate securities, and the limited liability feature, to be natural outgrowths facilitating corporate development.

> This organizational development which established procedures by which a corporate group of proprietors could appear in a court of law as a legal person, represented by its proper officials, was a product of practical business necessity. And the so-called personification of the stockholders together as a unit was a method by which the formal requirements of court procedure could be met. But this administrative machinery in itself could in no way alter the economic or legal status of the stockholders together as the owners of the enterprise, nor their responsibility to its creditors for any obligations incurred.[2]
> . . . .
> Without transferability of shares and the continuing sameness of the business entity, continuity and growth of the modern corporate enterprise would have been impossible. . . . But the magnitude of the growth of business enterprise made possible under the corporate form of organization must not be permitted to obscure the fact that the underlying proprietor-creditor relationships remained unchanged.[3]
> . . . .
> The net effect of the stockholders' limited liability feature in no way changed the nature of the proprietary position of the owners of the enterprise. The extent of their interest is still limited by the value of enterprise assets on the one hand and enterprise obligations on the other.[4]

Entity Theory of Accounting

The proprietary theory of accounting is by no means subscribed to by all accountants. In 1922, Paton attacked

[1]Maurice Moonitz and Charles C. Staehling, Accounting, An Analysis of Its Problems, Vol. I (Brooklyn: The Foundation Press, Inc., 1952), p. 11.

[2]Ibid., p. 12. [3]Ibid., p. 13. [4]Ibid., p. 14.

the proprietary approach to corporation accounting and proposed what has come to be known as the "entity theory" of
accounting.

> The technique of accounting has developed rapidly
> to meet the conditions of the large-scale enterprise,
> but theory--as is so often the case--has lagged far
> behind practice. In the case of the "single-proprie-
> torship," so-called, or the simple partnership, the
> proprietary is a fairly satisfactory pivotal category
> around which to construct the necessary accounting
> framework, but as an explanation of the accounting
> system of the corporation, the present dominant form
> of business organization, such an arrangement of
> accounting principles is seriously defective.
> . . .Accordingly an attempt has been made to pre-
> sent a restatement of the theory of accounting con-
> sistent with the conditions and needs of the business
> enterprise par excellence, the large corporation, as
> well as applicable to the simpler, more primitive
> forms of organization. The conception of the busi-
> ness enterprise as in all cases a distinct entity or
> personality--an extension of the fiction of the cor-
> porate entity--is adopted, although not without
> important qualifications.[1]

According to Littleton, there are some indications of
an entity theory to be found in medieval bookkeeping although
significant interest in the theory did not develop until
the nineteenth century, and in particular, about the last
quarter of the nineteenth century.[2] Among the more modern
accounting literature, Paton's Accounting Theory is generally credited as the first comprehensive exposition and
application of the entity theory as a basis for corporate
accounting analysis.

A concise statement of the basic premise of the
theory appears as one of the fundamental concepts upon

---

[1]Paton, op. cit., pp. iii-iv.

[2]Littleton, op. cit., chap. xii.

which Paton's and Littleton's highly regarded An Introduction to Corporate Accounting Standards is developed.

The business undertaking is generally conceived
of as an entity or institution in its own right,
separate and distinct from the parties who furnish
the funds, and it has become almost axiomatic that
the business accounts and statements are those of the
entity rather than those of the proprietor, partners,
investors, or other parties or groups concerned.[1]

As a separate and distinct entity, the corporation owns all the assets. There are, however, offsetting claims or rights. Paton calls these "equities," defining an equity as "a right in property."[2] This represents one of the distinguishing features of the entity theory: As it is usually conceived, the distinction between creditors and stockholders is largely abandoned. A stockholder is not an owner; he has merely an equity. And the same may be said of bondholders and other investors.

According to Paton, distinctions frequently made between stockholders and creditors are not fundamental distinctions but merely differences in degree.

The individual or interest that assumes the larger
element of risk in a business enterprise, and takes
the major share of responsibility and control, ap-
proximates the economist's "entrepreneur" and the
accountant's "proprietor"; the individual or interest
that furnishes capital but takes comparatively little
risk, and has but slight or indirect control of
ordinary operations, approaches the economist's
"capitalist proper" and the accountant's "creditor."
But it cannot be stated too emphatically that every
equity, proprietary or otherwise, furnishes capital
(money, commodities, or services); every equity involves risk of loss; virtually all equities have

[1] Paton and Littleton, op. cit., p. 8.

[2] Paton, op. cit., p. 38.

some privileges and responsibilities with respect to
management; and all long-term equities have rights
in income and capital.

To sum up: property ownership connotes such
attributes as control, title, risk-taking, and capital
furnishing. No one of these elements attaches ex-
clusively to what the accountant labels "proprietorship" as opposed to liabilities. Consequently we
can conclude that ownership or equities constitutes
a class rationally comprehending both of these
divisions.[1]

Paton refers to the entity theory as the "managerial

view, a conception of the corporation as a legal and eco-

nomic entity operating a mass of properties in the interest

of a whole body of investors of various classes."[2]

---

[1]Ibid., pp. 60-61.

[2]Ibid., p. 84. It is interesting to compare Paton's
early statements concerning the corporation and his more
recent statements. In Accounting Theory (1922) he wrote:
"The corporation, it may be reiterated, is the business
enterprise par excellence. In this case we have a genuine
business entity. The state endows the corporation with
attributes which give it an independent personality, an
existence apart and distinct from that of its individual
members. Limited liability and other significant consequences follow. Hence, for the accountant to view the corporation as a distinct institution, as having a real business
identity is thoroughly sound. No apology whatever need be
offered for this standpoint." (p. 68.)

In Essentials of Accounting (New York: The Macmillan
Company, 1938), Paton wrote: "Although it is the specific
business enterprise as a whole which represents the basic
unit of economic organization with which the accountant
deals, it must be recognized that in all forms of private
business activity the interests of the principal owners
or investors are dominant, at least as far as the accountant
is concerned. It is the owners or their employees who keep
the accounts; and it is primarily to serve the purposes of
the owners that accounts are maintained. The accountant,
therefore, inevitably views the business to a marked degree
from the point of view of the principal owners or proprietors. It is the records of the enterprise which he is
keeping and interpreting, but he is carrying on the work
at the direction of and to serve the needs of those who
furnish the capital and are in control" (p. 12).

In Essentials of Accounting (Revised ed.; New York:

In any event, the crux of the entity theory is the
separate and distinct nature of the corporate enterprise.[1]
Although his line of reasoning is couched in terms of "proprietorship," Canning also emphasizes this distinction

---

The Macmillan Company, 1949), he defines the corporation
as follows: "The corporation, like the firm, represents
an association of individuals or interests who have joined
their funds in a business undertaking with the hope of
making earnings. It has, however, certain distinctive and
important features" (p. 4). A discussion of the "features"
of legal entity, limited liability, transferability of
"corporate ownership," and transferability of "long-term
borrowing" follows.

Finally, in the first chapter, "Nature and Significance of Business Corporation," of Corporation Accounts
and Statements, published in 1955 "with the assistance of
William A. Paton, Jr.," Paton makes the following statement: "In some quarters there is a tendency to identify
the managerial group with the corporate entity, to regard
management as the ultimate source of responsibility for
corporate action. . . . This interpretation of the situation is not fundamentally sound or realistic. Hired managers may at times get the bit in their teeth and act as
if they could run the show as they see fit, but where this
condition develops management needs to be brought up with
a jerk, and the stockholders are negligent if they don't
see that this is done. To repeat, it is the stockholders,
not the executives, who possess the underlying authority
in corporate affairs. Managers are hired men, employees,
and they should realize this fact and be alert to the
interests of the investors (and the same thing may be
said of accountants). The business corporation is an
apparatus through which a group of people pool their resources for the purpose of carrying on some economic
activity; . . . (p. 6).

[1] One noteworthy exception to the usual accounting
use of the term "entity theory" is the "entity theory" of
consolidated statements advocated by Maurice Moonitz. In
direct contrast to the usual emphasis on the distinctiveness and separateness of a corporation and its stockholders
implied by the accounting use of the term "entity theory,"
Moonitz' use of the term symbolizes the obliteration of
legal distinctions and the recognition of the "economic
entity" which subsidiary corporations and their major (or
lone) stockholder, the parent holding company, comprise.
See Maurice Moonitz, The Entity Theory of Consolidated
Statements (Brooklyn: The Foundation Press, Inc., 1951).

between the corporation and its stockholders.

According to Canning, the term "proprietor" means
merely a "holder of assets." It is the corporation itself
which is the "holder of assets" and which is therefore the
proprietor. "The shareholders, as such, are proprietors
of their shares only--they have mere contracts with the
corporation in which certain beneficial interest in the
corporation's affairs are granted, for a consideration, to
subscribers and their successors."[1]

In the case of Canning, however, this emphasis upon
the separateness of the corporation and its shareholders
has not eliminated a significant distinction between creditors and shareholders. Canning's use of the term "proprietorship" refers to "the entire beneficial interest of a
holder of a set of assets in those assets" and is therefore equal to total assets (Assets = Proprietorship).
But Canning also distinguishes liabilities as a consideration which a proprietor (e.g., a corporation) is "under an
existing legal (or equitable) duty to render to a second
person (or set of persons)." The difference between gross
proprietorship (total assets) and liabilities is "net
proprietorship."[2] "Net proprietorship," then, is the
corporation's debt-free "estate in its assets," the

_____

[1]John B. Canning, The Economics of Accountancy (New
York: The Ronald Press Company, 1929), p. 55. For a comprehensive, critical review of Canning's concept of proprietorship, see Yee-Chuing Chow, "The Doctrine of
Proprietorship," The Accounting Review, XVII (April, 1942),
pp. 157-163.

[2]Ibid., pp. 55-56.

beneficial interest of which "lies entirely in the hands of shareholders."[1]

These distinctions may be clarified by the "test" Canning suggests:

> Rightly viewed, the question is not is the item under consideration a liability or a capital (net proprietorship) item; the significant inquiry is rather is the item a liability or not a liability? Is the claim represented adverse to the interest of the proprietor? Observe that the latter question is not is the result of the transaction out of which the claim arose adverse to the interest of the proprietor, but is the claim itself adverse to his interest?[2]

On the other hand, Canning suggests, the interests of <u>shareholders</u> are not "adverse" to the corporation (the "proprietor").

To paraphrase Canning in a few words, the claims of outsiders which are adverse to the corporation are liabilities; claims of outsiders which are consistent with the interests of the corporation comprise "net proprietorship"; the corporation itself is the proprietor of all the assets and is separate and distinct from those holding claims.

In Accounting Concepts of Profit, Stephen Gilman also discusses and adopts the entity theory. He does not limit its application to corporations but advocates its applicability wherever a double entry accounting record is maintained.[3] He views the corporation as an entity,

---

[1]<u>Ibid.</u>, p. 69.   [2]<u>Ibid.</u>, p. 61.

[3]Stephen Gilman, Accounting Concepts of Profit (New York: The Ronald Press Company, 1939), pp. 52-53.

separate and apart from the stockholders, whom he refers
to as "proprietors," but he does not look upon separateness and distinctiveness as unique features of the corporate
form of business organization. They are universal features,
for the purposes of accounting, of all forms of business
organization.

> . . . The proprietor is a person, or group, separate
> and distinct from the accounting entity; . . . the pro-
> prietor lends money to the accounting entity; . . . the
> accounting entity may or may not pay the money back to
> the proprietor, this being a matter determined by the
> proprietor's own wish and by any legal restrictions.
> Disregarding for the moment non-proprietorship
> liabilities, increases in entity property automatically
> become additional liabilities to the proprietor and
> decreases in property automatically reduce the lia-
> bility to the proprietor.[1]

It follows from this that "in and of itself the entity
makes no profits, suffers no losses."[2] "Profit is an increase in the amount the entity owes to the proprietor,
disregarding capital advances and withdrawals."[3]

In accounting, the entity theory has considerable
support. It is clear, however, that although there is
agreement among many accountants as to the fundamental concept of the corporation which is the basis for this theory
of accounting, the terminology and interpretations of the
implications of this concept are not in agreement.

According to Paton and Littleton, assets equal equities; there is no significant distinction to be made between
creditors and stockholders; and, "emphasis on the entity
point of view . . . requires the treatment of business

---

[1]Ibid., p. 52.   [2]Ibid., p. 52.   [3]Ibid., p. 48.

earnings as the income of the enterprise itself until such
time as transfer to individual participants has been effected by dividend declarations."[1]

According to Canning, assets equal proprietorship,
the corporation itself being the proprietor; creditors'
claims and claims against net proprietorship are distinctive; and income increases the debt-free estate of the
corporation in its assets.

And, according to Gilman, assets equal liabilities;
liabilities may be nonproprietorship liabilities or liabilities to proprietors but "it seems permissible to say
that from the viewpoint of the entity there is no distinction between the proprietor and other creditors,"[2] and
there can be no income of the enterprise itself.

Fund Theory of Accounting

In the late 1940's, Professor William J. Vatter, of
the University of Chicago, proposed a "fund theory" of
accounting. It would be inappropriate to consider Vatter's
fund theory as concerned strictly with a particular concept of the corporation; its scope is much broader. The
theory is held to be generally applicable to all forms of
business organization and to any kind or size of accounting
unit, whether more inclusive or less inclusive than what
is usually thought of as a "business organization." For

---

[1]Paton and Littleton, op. cit., p. 8.
[2]Gilman, op. cit., p. 51.

example, it is deemed to provide the basis for the accounting for departments within a corporation or for the accounting for a group of affiliated corporations on a consolidated basis. Basically, it is an extension of fund accounting as exemplified in governmental and eleemosynary institutions.

A fund is "the <u>unit</u> of accounting in the sense that it represents the field of attention covered by a given set of financial records and reports."[1] In accordance with the fund theory, the corporation is visualized as merely a fund or group of funds. Vatter explains, somewhat vaguely, that this concept lends greater objectivity to the accounting process.

> Neither the proprietary theory nor the entity theory is a wholly satisfying frame of reference for accounting. Each is vulnerable in that it adopts a personality as its focus of attention. The difference between them is mostly whether the person (for whom the books are kept and to whom the reports are made) is the "proprietor" or proprietors in their human selves, or whether real people must be viewed abstractly or in the guise of a fictional entity, corporate or otherwise. The weakness in these personalized bases for accounting is that the content of accounting reports will tend to be affected by personal analysis; and issues will be decided not by considering the nature of the problems but upon some extension of personality--to reach or to support conclusions that are for the most part mere expediencies. Dependence upon personality and personal implications in accounting theory, even as a convention, does not contribute to that objectivity toward which all quantitative analysis is aimed.[2]
>
> . . . .
> The notion of a fund has not been encumbered by personalistic thinking; it is free from those extensions of meaning which frequently creep into a theory based upon personalizations. And it is not bound up

[1]Vatter, <u>The Fund Theory of Accounting</u>, p. 12.
[2]<u>Ibid.</u>, p. 7.

with attitudes about valuation, the form and content
of financial reports, and related matters. There is
real advantage to be gained from an approach that
makes it possible to consider the problem of accounting from a fresh point of view--one which facilitates
the separation of issues now hopelessly bound together
in the personalistic systems of thought exemplified
by both proprietary and entity theories.[1]

The notion of the corporation as merely a "fund" is

not without some support in the legal literature. Taylor,

who feels the corporation may best be viewed as a set of

legal relations, wrote:

Corporate funds cannot with propriety be said to
be owned by anyone. . . . The result of the respective
rights of these different classes of persons is that
corporate property becomes a fund set apart for the
attainment of certain purposes from which it cannot
be diverted without the consent of all whose legally
protected interests would be injured by such diversion.[2]
. . . .
. . . A corporation, considered as a legal institution, is the sum of the legal relations resulting
from the operation of rules of law in its constitution
upon the various persons, who, by fulfilling the pre-
requisite conditions, bring themselves within the
operation of these rules. The general effect of these
legal relations is to convert the corporate funds, in
respect to which, through the operation of the constitution of the corporation, ownership properly speaking
ceases, into a 'fund for the attainment of the objects
of incorporation.[3]

In accordance with Vatter's fund theory, "assets are

economic in nature; they are embodiments of future want

satisfaction in the form of service potentials that may

be transformed, exchanged, or stored against future events."[4]

---

[1]Ibid., p. 13.

[2]Henry O. Taylor, op. cit., p. 24. For additional
reference to Taylor's views, see p. 35, supra.

[3]Ibid., p. 25.

[4]Vatter, The Fund Theory of Accounting, p. 17.

And a fund is a bundle of assets--a "collection of service potentials"--aggregated for a specific purpose. The assets of a corporation constitute such a fund (or funds).

Vatter also makes use of the term "equities" but redefines the term to designate "restrictions applicable to the assets in the fund."[1] This definition of equities is designed to eliminate the legal ramifications of the notion of "claims against assets" or "rights in property" and also to broaden the applicability of the term "equities" to embrace certain accounts found in institutional accounting.[2] Double-entry is based, therefore, on the equation "assets equal restrictions upon assets." The equality depends upon the notion of residual equity, "a final and pervasive restriction upon fund assets or any residual thereof, in the sense that the entire asset fund is confined to the set of operations for which the fund is established."[3]

Perhaps the most unusual aspect of the fund theory is the absence of a concept of income. Expense is described

---

[1]Ibid., p. 20.

[2]For example, "Reserve for Encumbrances." It is interesting to note that at least at one point Vatter resorts to the term "liabilities," presumably peculiar to the proprietary theory, in order to clarify the "restrictions" idea. "Applying the test of distributability to revenue is logically impossible, for it is not revenue but assets that are distributed. And, under legal notions of what constitutes proper dividend action, the amounts distributed must be unrestricted, that is, assets in excess of equity restrictions for liabilities, invested capital, and (as the statutes may happen to recognize them) certain kinds of surplus." Ibid., p. 37. One might ask if there are two classes of equity restrictions--for liabilities and for proprietorship?

[3]Ibid., p. 20.

as "a release of service to the designated objectives of
the fund."[1] This idea is meant to apply to nonprofit as
well as profit-seeking organizations and is therefore not
related to the earning of revenue. Revenue is the acquisition of new assets unaccompanied by equity restrictions
other than the residual equity. But no generally significant process of matching revenues and expenses is considered
feasible. Vatter rejects "the notion of income because of
the difficulties that arise from the personal associations
and interpretations that are embodied in such a concept as
can be evolved in operational terms."[2] Expense and revenue
accounts are used in the financial statements only to ex-
plain increases and decreases in the fund of assets.

Enterprise Theory of Accounting

Recently, it was suggested in an article appearing
in The Accounting Review that "both the structure and behavior of the large corporation are different from that
visualized under the 'proprietary' and 'entity' theories
of the firm."[3] Consequently it was proposed that, in the
case of the large corporation, an "enterprise theory" is
more appropriate. The large corporation is looked upon
as a "social institution" rather than as an entity or
association.

The development of this theory is based on the

---

[1]Ibid., p. 22. [2]Ibid., p. 38.
[3]Suojanen, op. cit., p. 391.

recognition in recent years on the part of the managements
of large corporations of the "social responsibilities of
the institutionalized corporation." Suojanen suggests
that such behavior is difficult to fit into the two traditional frames of reference found in accounting theory.

It should be noted at the outset that the applicability of this concept is limited to the "large" corporation.
"Large" corporations are defined as those "whose common
stock is listed on national or regional stock exchanges
and hence are subject to considerable degree of government
control."[1]

> In this concept, the enterprise is conceived as a
> decision-making center for the people who are partici-
> pants, however, /sic/ fleeting or intimate may be their
> contacts with it as an organization. The decisions
> made in the enterprise affect, in one way or another,
> the stockholders, the employees, the creditors, the
> customers, various governmental and social control
> agencies such as the Securities and Exchange Commission
> and the New York Stock Exchange, and that most ephemeral
> of groups known as the "public."[2]
> . . . .
> . . . . The industrial enterprise is the association
> through which the institution of the "new society" is
> made manifest. The concept of the enterprise is con-
> siderably broader than that of the entity because the
> former concept endeavors to discover the role of the
> firm as a self-contained abstraction existing apart
> from the rest of the community.[3]

According to this theory, management no longer represents the stockholders, but rather has become "the custodian"
of the enterprise. Many decisions are made in which the
interests of the stockholders are not paramount. Rather,
these decisions are dictated by the desire for growth and
survival of the enterprise as an organization.

---

[1]Ibid., p. 392. [2]Ibid., p. 392. [3]Ibid., p. 393.

This concept demands that accounting measure the contribution of the enterprise to society and Suojanen suggests a "value added" concept of income measurement for this purpose. The value added statement would analyze the value added in production and its source or distribution among the organization participants. The definition of "value added" developed by the Department of Commerce is proposed for this purpose: "Value added by manufacture is calculated by subtracting the cost of materials, supplies, and containers, fuel, purchased electric energy, and contract work from the total value of shipments."[1]

It is proposed that the value added statement be supplementary to the traditional type of income statements, and it is admitted that the preparation of such supplementary statement "need occasion no major reorientation of presently accepted accounting principles."[2] For the purposes of the value added statement, however, inventories would be valued at "selling price" rather than cost in order to emphasize production rather than sales.[3]

[1]U. S., Bureau of the Census, Census of Manufactures: 1947, I, 20.

[2]Suojanen, op. cit., p. 398.

[3]It may be noted that other accountants have recognized the virtue of using the "net realizable value" of inventories under some circumstances for income measurement and reporting purposes in conjunction with "traditional" theories of accounting. Cf. Reuel I. Lund, "Realizable Value As a Measurement of Gross Income," The Accounting Review, XXVI (December, 1941), 373-385. Net realizable value is selling price less costs of completion and disposal. The full "value" measured by selling price has not been "added" until the product is completed and delivered. One would expect, therefore, that Suojanen would also use net realizable value of inventories.

Using this approach, it is obvious that the wages
paid by the enterprise to its employees are of equal
significance, dollar for dollar, to dividends that are
distributed to the shareholders. The same reasoning
applies to income shares received by all the other participants in the enterprise, including the portion of
the earnings retained by the enterprise itself. Income
reporting on a "value added" basis recognizes that the
traditional, legal property rights have undergone a
change in the enterprise system and the rights of the
shareholders, like those of the other participants,
are subordinate to the viability of the enterprise
itself. It also recognizes that the responsibility of
the management is primarily that of preserving the
enterprise by mediating the claims of the organization
participants.[1]

Summary

The agreement among those in law who view the corporation as an association of individuals, those in economics
who look upon the common stockholder as the corporate entrepreneur, and those in accounting who advocate the proprietary theory is clear. Consistent application of this concept
by these three groups who are directly concerned with the
corporation is therefore feasible. The manifestation of
this concept in the accounting process will be examined
in detail in subsequent chapters.

There is likewise a consistent conceptual kinship
among those in law and accounting who view the corporation
as an entity quite separate and distinct from its shareholders and those in economics who place the entrepreneurial
function with the directors or officers or the corporation
itself. It was suggested earlier that the distinction

---

[1]Suojanen, op. cit., p. 398.

between the corporation and its stockholders would probably
require modification to preserve economic significance in
the case of parent and subsidiary relationships. Nevertheless, due to the popularity of the concept and the extent to which the concept does exist on common ground in
the areas of law, economics, and accounting, a more detailed
examination of its effect on accounting is merited.

It was previously concluded that if "corporation"
is merely a term for a particular set of legal relations,
it has no conceptual significance in economics or accounting. That conclusion is here reiterated. The elimination
of any significance of the concept of the corporation is
essentially the theme of Vatter's fund theory of accounting,
which focuses attention upon the assets brought together
as a fund to carry on specified activities. It is of no
particular importance whether the fund is utilized by a
proprietorship, partnership, nonprofit institution, or
business corporation; and in the case of the latter, therefore, it is likewise unimportant how the corporation-
stockholder relationship is viewed and who performs the
entrepreneurial function. In fact, Vatter proposes that
accounting information be provided in such a manner that
it may be rearranged by the user in a fashion which will
be consistent with the user's own concepts and purposes.

But the fund theory of accounting calls for the
recognition of restrictions imposed upon the use of the
fund of assets. Many of those restrictions are entirely

legal in character and must be determined by reference to
pertinent legal provisions. Accordingly, as the effects
of other concepts of the corporation on the accounting
analysis of specific transactions are examined, the accounting necessary to reflect purely the legal viewpoint will
be of interest.

The concept of the large corporation as a social
institution is quite in keeping with the concept of economic entity found in the legal literature. Suojanen's
enterprise theory of accounting and Berle's "enterprise
entity" deal essentially with the same concept. This
notion is likewise consistent with the writings of Dewing
and Berle and Means,[1] and much that has been said about
the entrepreneurial function in modern corporations. The
effect of this concept of the corporation, along with the
other concepts indicated above, constitutes the subject
matter of the remainder of this study.

---

[1]The views expressed by Berle, Dewing, and Berle
and Means are reviewed in chap. ii, supra.

CHAPTER V

THE EFFECT OF THE CONCEPT OF THE CORPORATION ON
THE ACCOUNTING FOR TRANSACTIONS INVOLVING
THE CORPORATION'S SECURITIES

Introduction

This chapter and the succeeding two chapters will
be concerned with the systematic examination of the effects
on accounting analysis of those concepts of the corporation which have been found to be significant in the fields
of law, economics, and accounting. The concepts which
seem to merit such detailed consideration are the corporation as an association of individuals, the corporation as
a separate and distinct entity, the corporation as merely
a particular set of legal relations, and the corporation
as a social institution.

The transactions for which the accounting might be
affected by the underlying concept of the corporation are
limited to transactions involving changes in the accounts
related to the interests of corporate security holders.
The accounting for exchanges of assets without gain or
loss and the accounting for transactions resulting in
equal increases or decreases in assets and short-term
creditors' accounts are not relevant and will not be considered.

It will be assumed that the concept of the corporation as an association of individuals requires that the common shareholders be considered tne **owners** of the corporate assets and **obligors** of the corporate debts, and that the legal entity of the corporation is a device of a representative nature by means of which the association's business affairs may be conveniently administered with certain legal privileges and within certain legal limitations. This notion suggests that accounts be constructed and maintained in such a way as to facilitate the preparation of financial reports for the common snareholders comprising the association.[1]

---

[1]This primary purpose of financial reports coincides with the view of the Committee on Concepts and Standards Underlying Corporate Financial Statements of the American Accounting Association:

"Since the ultimate test of the quality of any communication is its effectiveness in conveying pertinent information, the initial step in the development of standards of disclosure for published financial statements is the establishment of the purposes to be served. The potential users of corporate reports include governmental agencies, short- and long-term creditors, labor organizations, stockholders, and potential investors. Since in all likelihood tne needs of these groups cannot be served equally well by a single set of statements, the interest of some one audience should be identified as primary. Traditionally, this has been the stockholder group.

"In view of the facts that short-term creditors and governmental administrative agencies will typically have the power to require information specific to their purposes and that no important differences in the basic informational requirements of the other interests cited seem to exist, the traditional emphasis on the requirements of the stockholder group appears to be sound. In considering disclosure standards, therefore, the Committee has been concerned primarily with the use of financial statements (1) in the making of investment decisions and (2) in the exercise of investor control

The concept of separate and distinct corporate
existence will be interpreted to require that the corporation _itself_ be looked upon as the owner of the assets.
All outsiders with claims against the corporation are
grouped into one category--that of equityholders. Because
the corporate assets are owned by the corporation _itself_
and all corporate obligations are obligations of the corporation _itself_, there is no significant distinction to
be made between stockholders, bondholders, suppliers of
goods and services, and other obligees. In accordance with
this view, financial reports represent an accounting by the
corporation to all those having claims against it, i.e., to
all "equityholders."

It will be assumed here that the question of ownership of the corporation, viewed as a social institution,
is not of primary importance. The unique feature of this
concept lies in the assumed corporate objective of economic
growth and development in the interests of society. It is
to be noted that the incorporated social institution may
also be viewed separately and distinctly from the contributors of its capital. But, whereas the entity theory
of accounting has had as its established goal the financial reporting by the corporate entity to that entity's
investors, financial reports issued by the social institution should be directed to the public in general. And,

---

over management." "Standards of Disclosure for Published Financial Reports," _The Accounting Review_,
XXX (July, 1955), p. 401.

although the incorporated social institution must be operated within a legal framework, data concerning the corporation's legal status would seem to be clearly secondary to information concerning its general economic status.

Use of the term "corporation" to indicate a prescribed set of legal relations obviates the identification of ownership of corporate assets. The corporate assets may properly be looked upon as simply a "fund" made available for the accomplishment of the objectives of incorporation. The uses of such assets are limited by restrictions applicable to the assets, the restrictions being essentially legal in nature or imposed by management with legal approbation. The attainment of the corporate objectives must be fulfilled within the limitations imposed by such restrictions and, accordingly, this concept of the corporation requires that the accounts be maintained in conformity with the statutory provisions of the state of incorporation.

In this study, no attempt will be made to examine all state statutes and thereby exhaust all possible legal interpretations. Reference will be made to the Minnesota Business Corporations Act and the California Corporations Code, however, in order that the legal effects in those states, at least, can be contrasted with the effects of the analyses consistent with other corporate concepts.

Capital Stock Transactions

Issuance of capital stock--in general: When capital stock is originally issued in exchange for assets, an accounting

for the increase in stockholders' investment and the increase
in assets is required.[1] The capital stock may have a par
value or it may have no par value, but where the latter is
the case the statutes of the state of incorporation generally provide that a _stated_ value may, within limits, be
arbitrarily designated by the board of directors. In the
absence of such designation, the entire consideration is
the stated value.[2] The significance of the stated value
of no-par capital stock is identical to that of par value:
an amount equal to the total of the par or stated values
of issued shares, sometimes referred to as the _stated_
capital or _legal_ _capital_, is, in general, not legally available for dividends. It is intended that creditors be able
to look upon the legal capital as a form of protection for
their (the creditors') interests in the assets of the corporation. The legal capital represents a "cushion" for
absorption of corporate losses preceding any impairment
of the creditors' interests.

Where the consideration received by the issuing corporation is equal to the par or stated value, the economic
significance and the legal significance of the transaction
are identical. Where the consideration received is in

---

[1]Subscriptions for capital stock may precede the
actual issuance of stock certificates but what is said
here about _issuance_ of capital stock is meant to embrace
the subscription process.

[2]See for example, _Minnesota Business Corporation Act_
(1933), s. 301.21, and _California Corporations Code_ (1947),
s. 1900(b). These statutes will subsequently be referred
to as _Minn._ and _Calif._, respectively.

excess of the par or stated value, from the economic viewpoint the excess and the par or stated value are homogeneous--
the entire amount is the stockholders' investment. But, from
the legal viewpoint, careful distinction between the par
or stated value and the excess may be required. In some
states, under certain prescribed conditions, dividends may
be legally declared to the extent of amounts received in
excess of the stated or par value of capital stock issues.[1]
This excess is therefore described as "paid-in surplus."
It is "paid in" by the original purchasers of the stock
issue, and it is "surplus" in the sense that it represents
an amount over and above the legal capital required to be
retained by the corporation for the protection of creditors.

It is possible that par value stock be originally
issued at a "discount," that is, for a consideration less
than the par value. In some states, however, the issuance
of capital stock at a discount is prohibited by statute.[2]
Typically, the stated values designated for no-par stock
must be equal to or less than the consideration received.[3]

---

[1]Minn., s. 301.22 and Calif., s. 1500(c).

[2]Minn., s. 301.15, subd. 3. In California, "a corporation may issue par value shares, as fully paid up, at
less than par, if the board of directors determines that
such shares cannot be sold at par." Calif., s. 1110.

[3]Minn., s. 301.21 and Calif., s. 1900(b). There are
also other limitations on the designation of stated value.
In Minnesota, if no-par stock has a liquidation preference,
only that part of the consideration which is in excess of
such liquidation preference may be designated paid-in surplus. Otherwise, any part of the consideration may be
designated as paid-in surplus. Minn., s. 301.21, subd. 3.
In California, "the entire amount of the agreed consideration

Where that is the law, a "discount" on no-par stock is not possible.

Whatever the amount of consideration, from an economic viewpoint it constitutes the original stockholders' investment. Discount may have legal significance, nevertheless, for in some states stockholders and directors may be held personally liable for amounts equal to discounts on shares where such individuals were aware of the discounts and where these amounts are required in order to satisfy prior claims.[1]

It is customary in recording increases in stockholders' investment to recognize the legal distinctions described above. Where the consideration received by the issuing corporation is in excess of the par or stated value, the increase in stockholders' investment is recorded in two accounts--one for the par or stated value and one for the excess, frequently referred to as "premium." And in those states where discount has significance, it is customary to record the increase in legal capital, usually represented by a "capital stock" account, in the amount of the par value and to record the amount of the discount in a separate account. The balance of the latter account then represents a partial offset to the account containing legal capital and is said to be a "contra" or "valuation"

for shares without par value having a liquidation preference shall be credited to stated capital." _Calif._, s. 1900(b).

[1]_Minn._, s. 301.15, subd. 4.

account. The difference between the capital stock account
and the discount account represents the consideration contributed by the original purchasers of such stock.

It is reported[1] that there has been some tendency,
particularly in the past, to look upon discount on par
value stock as an asset. In states such as Minnesota,
where those who purchase par value shares at a discount
and subsequent transferees with notice are "liable to the
corporation" for the amount of the discount, it is not
entirely unreasonable to look upon that discount as a form
of receivable. The extreme circumstances under which collection of the amount of the discount might be undertaken
and the degree of uncertainty with respect to its ultimate
collectibility, however, seem to render such a "receivable"
valueless, or nearly so. It would appear, therefore, to
be more realistic to utilize the information contained in
the "discount on capital stock" account to disclose the
portion of legal capital actually contributed to the corporation by stockholders in the form of cash or other
valuable assets. Today, there seems to be general agreement with this view. In any event, as suggested by Finney
and Miller, "With the advent of no-par stock, the question
of the treatment of stock discount has become almost

_____

[1]See H. A. Finney and Herbert E. Miller, Principles
of Accounting, Intermediate (4th ed.; New York: Prentice-
Hall, Inc., 1951), p. 242; Moonitz and Staehling, op. cit.
II, 97; W. A. Paton (ed.), Accountants' Handbook (3d ed.;
New York: The Ronald Press Company, 1943), p. 1001; and
Paton and Paton, op. cit., p. 58.

entirely academic, for a company with stock discount on
its books is a rarity."[1] Similarly, recent use of low
par value stocks (e.g., \$1 to \$10 per share) is apt to
help render stock discount extinct.

Issuance of capital stock--common: There is nothing inherent in the association of individuals concept or the
concept of separate and distinct entity which demands the
segregation of par or stated values of common stock from
paid-in surplus derived from common stock issues. The
entire consideration, whatever the amount, represents the
investment of the owners and entrepreneurs associated in
a business venture or the equity of capitalists investing
in a legal entity separate and distinct from themselves,
depending on the view favored.

The source of corporate capital (assets) would also
seem to be fundamental information if the corporation is
to be looked upon as a social institution. The legal
ramifications are of relatively little significance except
to those charged with the regulation of corporate activities and those responsible for complying with such regula-
tions.

The concept of the corporation as a set of legal
relations, however, requires the recognition of the legal
distinction between par or stated value and premium and
discount. The fund theory of accounting, which seems to
be consistent with the strictly legal concept of the

[1]Finney and Miller, op. cit., p. 242.

corporation, requires an accounting recognition of such
legal distinctions because the legal "restrictions" represented by the par or stated value of capital stock differ
significantly from the legal "restrictions" represented by
paid-in surplus.

On the other hand, the recognition of the legal distinctions need not necessarily be antagonistic to the
association, separate entity, or social institution concepts. The following information is consistent with all
four of the corporate concepts under consideration.

> Common stock: authorized, 100,000 shares; no par
> value; stated value, ₩10 per share. All shares
> are issued and outstanding.

Designated as legal capital	$1,000,000
Consideration received in excess of designated legal capital	1,500,000
Total investment contributions of common shareholders	₩2,500,000

Issuance of capital stock--preferred: Where different
classes of stock are issued, separate accounts are required
to some extent, regardless of the corporate concept.
Investments in preferred stock are not homogeneous with
investments in common stock. Although both kinds of stock
may be held by one individual, the natures of the investments differ. Typically, dividends in a specified amount
must be paid to preferred shareholders before dividends
may be paid to common shareholders and, in the event of
liquidation, the claims of preferred shareholders have
priority over the claims of common shareholders. Also,

voting rights are usually not extended to preferred shareholders except in certain circumstances such as in the
absence of the declaration of preferred dividends for some
specified period of time.[1]

From the association viewpoint, preferred shareholders cannot be considered "co-owners" with the common
shareholders. The investment risks and rewards are not
the same. Economists who place the entrepreneurial activity
with the common shareholders implicitly exclude preferred
shareholders.[2] It would not be consistent with the association of individuals concept to intermingle completely
these two types of investments.

Similarly, investments in common and preferred stock
are distinguishable from the entity viewpoint. As a separate and distinct entity the corporation has different
obligations to preferred shareholders and common shareholders. The natures of their "equities" are not identical.

It is also clear that the different legal characteris-
tics of common and preferred stock require separate accounting if the strictly legal point of view is to be represented.

---

[1]In a study of the contract provisions of 72 preferred
stocks issued during the period 1946 to 1950, it was found
that in every case there was a cumulative preference as to
dividends and a preference as to assets in the event of
liquidation. Of the 72 issues, only 13 granted general voting
rights while 62 granted voting rights contingent on the omis-
sion of dividends. The 13 issues granting general voting
power were restricted "largely" to corporations operating
within the influence of unique statutory provisions of the
state of Illinois. Donald A. Fergusson, "Recent Developments
in Preferred Stock Financing," The Journal of Finance, VII
(September, 1952), pp. 447-462.

[2]See chap. iii, supra.

Premium received upon the issuance of preferred
stock, however, is not legally distinguishable from premium
received upon the issuance of common stock. That is to say,
the "restrictions" represented by premium on stock are
identical regardless of source. Accordingly, it is acceptable from the legal point of view to use a single paid-in
surplus account for amounts received in excess of par or
stated value of either preferred or common stock.

Although in the case of common stock issues it is
not necessary to separate premium from legal capital in
order to manifest the association or proprietary point of
view, it is necessary to make that kind of distinction in
connection with preferred stock issues. The criterion here
is ownership and amounts received in excess of par or stated
value, although paid in by investors in preferred stock,
increase the common shareholders' ownership.

The same holds true with respect to the separate and
distinct corporate entity existing and operating for the
benefit of all its investors. The corporation owns all
the assets but the total of its assets is always equal to
the total equities--"the claims against or rights in"[1] its
assets. Consideration received in excess of par or stated
value of preferred stock issues becomes part of the equity
of common shareholders.[2]

---

[1]Paton, Accounting Theory, p. 37.

[2]It must be acknowledged that the determination of
equities and ownership is necessarily based to a considerable degree on legal interpretations.

Some of those who advocate the entity theory of accounting do not agree with this analysis. Paton and
Littleton write:

> . . . If par-value preferred stock is issued at a
> premium, the premium may be considered at law to be a
> form of surplus attaching to the equity of the common
> shareholder. Indeed, it may not be illegal to appropri-
> ate such premium as dividends on common stock. This
> position does not harmonize with accounting standards;
> for accounting purposes the entire amount paid in by
> the preferred stockholders should be reported as pre-
> ferred stock equity. . . .The accountant should report
> the amount paid in as the recognizable equity.[1]

It is here submitted that such reporting is inconsistent. The accountant may report the amount <u>paid in</u> by
preferred shareholders or the <u>equity</u> of preferred shareholders, but, where preferred stock is issued at a premium,
these two amounts are not necessarily the same.

In <u>Corporation Accounts and Statements</u>, with respect
to this question, Paton and Paton declare:

> The position is taken here that it is the business of
> the accountant to report clearly and separately the
> amount invested by each class of investors. . . . This
> treatment is sound even if the equity of the preferred
> shares in the event of liquidation is more or less
> than the amount paid in. . . . The initial fact of
> importance with respect to the preferred stock, cer-
> tainly, is the amount received from the preferred stock-
> holders. And call price and contractual rights in
> liquidation continue to remain in the status of supple-
> mentary data unless and until redemption is decided
> upon or liquidation becomes imminent.[2]

It is agreed that "this treatment is sound" provided
no pretense is made that the accounts disclose the <u>equity</u>
of preferred shareholders. At no time do preferred shareholders

[1]Paton and Littleton, <u>op. cit.</u>, p. 42.

[2]Paton and Paton, <u>op. cit.</u>, p. 81.

have a valid "claim against" the assets of the corporation
or "rights in" the corporation's assets in the amount of
the premium.

There may be a liquidation preference which is greater
than par value, but the difference between par and such
preference constitutes an increment of ownership or equity
which is contingent upon liquidation.[1] Under normal circumstances, the amount of liquidation preference may be
excluded from the accounts on the grounds that the accounts
are intended to reflect the status of a continuing business
unit. From this "going concern" point of view, liquidation

---

[1]Studies indicate that the preference afforded holders
of par value preferred shares in the event of involuntary
liquidation (as a result of financial difficulty) is usually
in the amount of the par value or par value and accumulated
dividends. Of 752 par value preferred stock issues which
had liquidation preferences on New York Stock Exchange
listing applications between 1885 and 1934, 597 were preferred in involuntary liquidation in the amount of par or
par and accumulated dividends. Another 149 called for a
fixed premium in addition to the par or par and accumulated
dividends in the event of involuntary liquidation. Of the
752, 290 called for a fixed premium in addition to the par
or par and accumulated dividends in the event of voluntary
(as a result of a resolution adopted by shareholders
accorded voting power) liquidation. W. H. S. Stevens,
"Stockholders' Participation in Assets in Dissolution,"
The Journal of Business of the University of Chicago, X
(January, 1937), 49.

Based on his study of 72 preferred stocks issued
during the period 1946 to 1950, Fergusson generalized as
follows: "All the preferred stocks investigated have a
liquidation preference over the common. All are callable
at a decreasing premium over par value or offering price.
In the event of voluntary liquidation the amount of the
preference is usually par value plus accumulated dividends
plus a premium based on the current redemption price of the
stock. In involuntary liquidation the premium is omitted."
Fergusson, op. cit., p. 459.

preferences have no significance. A corporation facing
liquidation proceedings, whether it be voluntary or involuntary, constitutes a special case.

The par or stated value of outstanding preferred
stock is the basic equity of preferred shareholders. That
is the amount which is protected from impingement to the
benefit of junior security holders. In this study the concept of the corporation as a separate and distinct entity
is assumed to call for a periodic accounting by the corporation to its equityholders. In accordance with this
concept it is proposed that premium on preferred stock
issues be labeled "consideration received in excess of par
(or stated) value of preferred stock" and be shown as a
component of the common shareholders' equity.

On the other hand, the source of the capital of the
corporation, viewed as a social institution, is most relevant. Accounts should be maintained to provide information
concerning the assets derived from the issuance of preferred
stock as one kind of risk and investment, perhaps meriting
one level of return, and to provide information concerning
the assets derived from the issuance of common stock as an
investment of a significantly different type, perhaps
deserving quite a different range of returns. The inter-
mingling of amounts invested in preferred stock with amounts
invested in common stock merely because they are in excess
of an artificial legal designation does not appear to be
consistent with this concept.

Illustrations of the type of information each of
the four concepts of the corporation seems to _require_ are
presented below. The data contained in each of these
illustrations are assumed to be based on identical transactions. It is to be noted that the information consistent
with the association and entity concepts differs only as
to terminology.

Illustration 1

Association of Individuals Concept

Preferred stock: authorized, 10,000 shares;
6% cumulative; par value, $100; liquidation
preference in the amount of par and accumulated
dividends. All shares are issued and outstanding. No dividends are in arrears.

    Total par value $1,000,000

Proprietorship:

    Common stock: authorized, 100,000 shares;
        no par value; stated value, $10 per share.
        All shares are issued and outstanding.

    Total investment contributions of
        common shareholders $2,500,000

    Consideration received in excess of
        par value of preferred stock   100,000

    Accumulated undistributed earnings   400,000

        Total proprietorship   3,000,000

           Total $4,000,000

Illustration 2

Concept of Separate and Distinct Entity

Preferred shareholders' equity:

Preferred stock: authorized, 10,000 shares;
6,5 cumulative; par value, ₩100; liquidation preference in the amount of par and
accumulated dividends. All shares are
issued and outstanding. No dividends are
in arrears.

Total par value   ₩1,000,000

Common shareholders' equity:

Common stock: authorized, 100,000 shares;
no par value; stated value, ₩10 per
share. All shares are issued and
outstanding.

Total investment contributions
    of common shareholders   ₩2,500,000

Consideration received in excess
of par value of preferred
stock   100,000

Accumulated undistributed earnings   400,000

Total common shareholders'
    equity   3,000,000

    Total   4,000,000

Illustration 3

Corporation as a Set of Legal Relations

Legal capital:

Preferred stock: authorized, 10,000 shares;
6,o cumulative; par value, ₀100; liquidation preference in the amount of par and
accumulated dividends. All shares are
issued and outstanding. No dividends are
in arrears.

Total par value	₀1,000,000

Common stock: authorized, 100,000 shares;
no par value; stated value, ₀10 per
share. All shares are issued and
outstanding.

Total stated value	1,000,000
Total legal capital	₀2,000,000
Paid-in surplus	1,600,000
Earned surplus	400,000
Total	₀4,000,000

Illustration 4

Corporation as a Social Institution

Sources

Preferred stock: authorized, 10,000 shares;
6,5 cumulative; par value, $100; liquidation
preference in the amount of par and accumulated dividends. All shares are issued and
outstanding. No dividends are in arrears.

Capital derived from preferred stock issues $1,100,000

Common stock: authorized, 100,000 shares; no
par value; stated value, $10 per share.
All shares are issued and outstanding.

Capital derived from common stock issues   2,500,000

Accumulated undistributed earnings   400,000

   Total $4,000,000

Purchase of treasury stock: Treasury stock is capital
stock which a corporation has issued and subsequently reacquired and which has not been formally canceled or formally
restored to a status of authorized but unissued. Consequently, treasury shares have the unique legal status of
shares which have been issued but which are not outstanding.
The gratuitous acquisition of treasury shares will be considered in Chapter VII in conjunction with other types of
donations. The purchase of treasury stock results in a
decrease in the assets given in consideration; the corres-
ponding effect upon appropriate accounts is the subject at
hand.

The legal interpretation of treasury stock transactions must be based on the statutes of the state of incorporation, and these statutes are apt to differ significantly
with regard to the purchase and reissue or retirement of
treasury shares.

In Minnesota, treasury shares may be purchased only
"out of" earned surplus or paid-in surplus. That is to
say, the amount of assets which may legally be used by a
corporation to reacquire its own outstanding stock is
limited to an amount equal to paid-in and/or earned surplus.
But, where there is preferred stock outstanding, only such
preferred stock may be purchased "out of" paid-in surplus.[1]

The California statute is somewhat more specific and,
with respect to paid-in surplus, more restrictive. It may

---

[1] Minn., s. 301.22, subd. 6.

be said that as a general rule, in California, paid-in
surplus may not be diminished upon the purchase of a corporation's own stock even if there is only one class outstanding. The statute lists five specific exceptions to
this general rule. Shares may also be purchased "out of"
stated capital under the same five conditions.[1] There is
also an additional classification of surplus in California--
reduction surplus--which may be "used" for the purchase of
preferred shares or for the purchase of common stock where
it is the only class outstanding.[2] The "use" of earned
surplus for the purchase of treasury stock is unrestricted.[3]

Reduction surplus results from the formal legal process
prescribed for the reduction of legal capital, paid-in surplus has been described earlier, and earned surplus represents
the accumulated amount of undistributed earnings (as in
contrast to investment contributions). Again, these are
"surplus" in the sense that they represent amounts over and
above the stated capital required to be retained by the corporation. It is intended that limiting the use of assets
for the purchase of treasury shares by the amount of surplus
will assure that the mere reacquisition of a corporation's
own shares cannot reduce the corporation's stated capital
and thereby unduly weaken that protection afforded creditors
and preferred shareholders.

Because the purchase of treasury shares does not

---

[1] Calif., s. 1706.   [2] Ibid., s. 1906.
[3] Ibid., s. 1707(c).

reduce stated capital, the capital stock account (in which
has been recorded the stated capital derived from original
stock issues) is unaffected. Moreover, since treasury
shares have a legal status which is different from that
of unissued shares and issued and outstanding shares, it
is appropriate that a separate accounting be made for treasury
stock. The balance of the treasury stock account then represents a decrease in earned surplus, paid-in surplus, reduction
surplus, or some combination of the three, depending upon
the state's legal provisions and the whim of the board of
directors. It is probably inexpedient to reduce the surplus
accounts directly. The treasury stock purchase should be
shown in the financial statements as a change (decrease) in
the relevant surplus account, and the treasury stock account
will provide the information concerning the magnitude of
that change.

One suggested procedure for accounting for the purchase
of treasury shares is to consider the treasury stock account
as an offset or reduction from the total of the accounts
containing stated capital and the accounts containing surplus. In conjunction with this procedure, an amount of
surplus equivalent to the cost of the treasury stock is
earmarked or segregated to indicate that amount is no longer
available for dividends or no longer free from legal restrictions.[1] From a legal point of view this procedure does not
seem to be acceptable. There is in general no legal

---

[1]Finney and Miller, op. cit., pp. 285-287.

justification for considering the cost of treasury stock
to be a deduction from the accounts containing stated capital. Furthermore, the purchase of treasury stock does not
act merely to "freeze" or restrict the related amount of
surplus which is, by definition, an amount over and above
stated capital; surplus is actually reduced. And this
legal result is not changed by substituting the term
"retained earnings" for earned surplus. Undistributed
earnings which have been "used" to purchase treasury shares
are not merely earmarked or frozen; they have been diminished;
they are no longer retained.[1]

From the standpoint of an association of individuals,
the purchase of association members' common stock by the
remaining co-owners constitutes a reduction in proprietorship. The purchase of the association's own preferred
stock constitutes the redemption of a senior security.
Since the legal status of the association is not deemed to
be the primary consideration, it would seem appropriate in
either case to reduce the accounts containing the relevant
type of investment contribution.

---

[1]It has even been suggested that the segregation of
an appropriate portion of surplus is unnecessary; that when
balance sheets are prepared, a footnote explanation is
satisfactory. Ibid., p. 237.

Such a footnote, however, would seem to contradict
the information in the body of the statement. The footnote
would necessarily point out that the corporation's surplus
or earnings retained in the corporation is overstated. Since
legal capital is not affected, it would seem that surplus
or retained earnings could remain undiminished, where assets
are given in consideration for treasury stock, only if
treasury stock itself is an asset. This is generally recognized not to be the case.

If a consideration greater than par or stated value
is given for the reacquisition of preferred shares, that
excess constitutes a type of "bonus" or "dividend" provided by the owners (common shareholders) and presumably
required by market conditions in order to induce the preferred shareholders to relinquish their shares. And, since
both accumulated undistributed earnings and consideration
received in excess of par or stated value of preferred
stock are components of the common shareholders' total proprietorship, it might be argued that it is immaterial which
of these accounts is reduced by the amount of the "bonus"
or "dividend." However, preferred shareholders who are
forced into "retirement" can hardly receive a bonus distribution of earnings before their original investment contribution is completely returned. Accordingly, any portion
of the account containing "excess consideration" which was
derived from the original issue of the reacquired preferred
shares should first be eliminated. Any further amount in
excess of the par or stated value and the related premium
should then be considered a distribution of earnings to
the preferred shareholder. The over-all effect of this
procedure is to withdraw from the accounts the entire
investment contribution originally received in consideration for the now reacquired preferred shares and to reduce
accumulated undistributed earnings by the amount of the

"dividend" paid at the time of reacquisition.[1]

The same general procedure applies to the reacquisition of common shares. The transaction should be analyzed so as to reflect in the accounts the withdrawal of the entire original investment contribution received in consideration for the reacquired common shares and the distribution of a "dividend," if any, "out of" earnings in conjunction with the reacquisition.[2]

If the consideration given for preferred treasury shares is less than par or stated value, the preferred stock account should still be reduced by the full par or stated value. The difference constitutes an addition to the common shareholders' proprietorship and represents a financial gain on the retirement of preferred stock. Where common shares are reacquired at a cost less than par or stated value, the cost should merely be deducted from "total investment contributions of common shareholders."

According to the concept of separate and distinct entity it is the corporation itself which reacquires outstanding shares of stock rather than the remaining co-owners

---

[1]Accounting for the purchase of treasury stock in this manner is in accordance with the procedure recommended by the Executive Committee of the American Accounting Association. Accounting Concepts and Standards Underlying Corporate Financial Statements (1948 Revision; American Accounting Association), pp. 5-6.

[2]It is recognized that this procedure does not conform to the law. It is assumed, however, the proprietors expect economic and financial information from accountants and will turn to lawyers for legal information. It is further assumed that accountants are better qualified to analyze the economic effects of transactions than to determine legal effects.

of the association. The effect of the transaction is a reduction of shareholders' equities. The accounting for the transaction, however, is like that which is consistent with the association of individuals concept. The transaction should be analyzed so as to reflect in the accounts a reduction of all or the appropriate part of the investment contribution received at the time of the original issue of the shares of stock which are now reacquired. Where the cost of treasury shares exceeds that original investment contribution, the excess constitutes an allotment of a portion of the accumulated undistributed earnings. If the original investment contribution was greater than the reacquisition cost, the difference remains as investment contributions of shareholders albeit this difference is now "in excess of the par or stated value" of the outstanding shares of the relevant class of stock.[1]

Because the accounts of the corporation as a social institution should be maintained to provide information primarily of an economic nature, there are no classifications of surplus, ownership, or equities to complicate the analysis of treasury stock transactions. The reacquisition of outstanding shares constitutes a withdrawal of capital derived from the issue of the stock in question and, if

---

[1]This analysis agrees basically with that of Paton and Littleton. However, they suggest different accounting treatment for "reissuable" treasury shares and shares which "are not reissuable." But this distinction appears to be based on bookkeeping convenience rather than any concept of the corporation or "corporate accounting standard." Paton and Littleton, op. cit., pp. 115-116.

the amount of assets given in reacquisition exceeds the
amount received when the stock was originally issued, a
distribution of accumulated earnings is made simultaneously
with the withdrawal.

Presumably, the reacquisition cost exceeds the original
investment contribution because the shares of stock in question have appreciated in dollar market value. This appreciation may be due to the accumulation of undistributed earnings,
an increase in the price level, a predicted prosperous
future, or some combination of equally intangible influences.
If the basis for the appreciation proves to have been justified, ultimately it will be reflected in the corporation's
operations and consequently in the accumulated undistributed
earnings account. It is therefore deemed appropriate that
the payment for "appreciation" of reacquired shares be considered a reduction of that account. If the amount of
assets invested at the time of original issue exceeds the
amount withdrawn, the difference is still properly classified in the account for capital derived from the issue of
the appropriate class of stock.

Retirement of treasury stock: Treasury shares may be
held "in the treasury" indefinitely or may ultimately be
disposed of in one of two ways: (1) they may be formally
retired, possibly reverting to a status of authorized and
unissued, or (2) they may be returned to an issued and
outstanding status by reissuance.

Formal retirement must be accomplished in conformity

with the provisions of the statutes of the state of incorporation. In Minnesota, preferred shares may be formally retired and the related stated capital reduced by resolution of the board of directors. This provision is straightforward. The statute provides further that:

> . . . Articles of reduction of stated capital . . . shall be executed and filed for record . . . and upon the recording thereof by the secretary of state the reduction of stated capital shall become effective. As soon as said articles of reduction shall have become effective any such shares . . . shall have the status of authorized and unissued shares of the class to which such shares belong.[1]

There is no specific provision in Minnesota, however, for the reversion of reacquired common shares to a status of authorized and unissued. But, within certain prescribed limitations the stated capital, represented by the par or stated value of issued common stock, may be reduced by a resolution "adopted by the vote of the holders of a majority in interest of the shares entitled to vote thereon" to an amount not less than "the sum of the par value of all outstanding shares having a par value and the aggregate amount to which outstanding shares without par value are entitled upon involuntary liquidation in preference to shares of another class or classes."[2] Any such reduction in stated capital becomes paid-in surplus.[3]

To summarize Minnesota treasury stock transactions involving common shares, where a corporation has issued stock which is preferred in liquidation as well as common

---

[1]Minn., s. 301.39, subd. 1. [2]Ibid., s. 301.39, subd. 2.
[3]Ibid., s. 301.21, subd. 4.

stock, the common shares can be reacquired, but only "out of" earned surplus. And, upon the adoption of a resolution by the vote of the majority of the holders of common stock, an appropriate amount of the par or stated value of the reacquired common shares may be transferred to paid-in surplus. Such paid-in surplus, however, is "available for dividends" to the preferred stockholders only. It appears that in this situation a "formal retirement" of common treasury shares would not be particularly popular and might well take place only if to do so would facilitate the legal declaration of dividends on the remaining outstanding shares of common stock.[1] However, if a corporation has no preferred stock, under the Minnesota statute common stock can be reacquired and stated capital reduced by the prescribed procedure with the result that the transfer to paid-in surplus does again "make available for dividends" to the remaining common shareholders that part of the cost of the treasury stock represented by its par or stated value.

The provisions of the <u>California</u> <u>Corporations</u> <u>Code</u> are roughly the same. There is, however, a blanket provision that "treasury shares may be retired and restored to the status of authorized and unissued shares without reduction of stated capital."[2] And, by properly approved

---

[1]For example, assume there is no paid-in surplus and only sufficient earned surplus for the desired dividends on common stock. This transfer from common stock legal capital to paid-in surplus could make dividends on both preferred and common stock legal.

[2]<u>Calif.</u>, s. 1714.

resolution, stated capital may be reduced to an amount not
"less than the aggregate par value of all par value shares
without liquidation preference to remain outstanding after
such reduction and the aggregate amount of the liquidation
preferences upon involuntary liquidation of preferred shares
with or without par value to remain outstanding after such
reduction."[1] Any such reduction in stated value constitutes
"reduction surplus" which may, in turn, be diminished by
the declaration of preferred dividends or purchase of outstanding preferred shares or, if there is only one class
of stock outstanding, by the declaration of dividends to
holders of that stock or the purchase of shares of that
stock.[2] Shares purchased "out of" stated capital "are
restored to the status of authorized but unissued shares"[3]
and shares purchased "out of" reduction surplus "are restored
to the status of authorized but unissued shares without
reduction of stated capital."[4]

If the purchase of treasury stock has been accounted
for in the manner previously described as consistent with
the association of individuals concept, the concept of
separate and distinct entity, and the social institution
concept, a subsequent formal retirement will not affect
any of the related accounts. Only the descriptive information concerning the number of shares issued and outstanding
is changed.

[1]Ibid., s. 1904. [2]Ibid., s. 1906.
[3]Ibid., s. 1710. [4]Ibid., s. 1711.

Reissuance of treasury stock: Treasury shares are frequently acquired with the intent of reissuing them, e.g.,
in connection with an employee stock purchase plan. From
the viewpoint of an association of individuals, the reissuance of treasury stock is analogous to an original issue
of capital stock. The sale of preferred stock creates an
obligation of the association evidenced by securities
senior to those denoting ownership (common stock); the
sale of common stock constitutes additional ownership investment. The effects of treasury stock issues upon the accounts
of the association are the same as those previously described
for the original issuance of capital stock. It is immaterial
whether or not the shares have been formally retired and
have legally reverted to an authorized and unissued status.

The same may be said of the effects of the reissuance of treasury stock on the accounts of the separate
and distinct corporate entity and the incorporated economic
social institution. From the viewpoint of the former concept, the issue of treasury stock creates an equity in
favor of the purchaser; in the case of the latter concept,
the proceeds of a treasury stock issue constitute capital
derived from stock issues.

As a set of legal relations, a corporation's accounts
are affected by the legal ramifications of the transaction
involving the reissuance of treasury stock. It is to be
noted that if the treasury shares have been formally
retired and have reverted to a status of authorized and
unissued, legally they are no longer considered treasury

116

shares and the effect of their reissuance is the same as
for other authorized and unissued shares.

The Minnesota Business Corporation Act has no specific
provision dealing with the treatment of the reissue of
treasury shares except that such shares may be issued for
a consideration less than par or stated value.[1] In the
absence of any provision to the contrary and because the
purchase of treasury stock does not reduce legal capital,
it seems reasonable that the reissuance of treasury stock
should not increase legal capital.

It is frequently urged that accounts reduced by the
acquisition of treasury stock are replenished by its reissue.
Marple, for example, says, "In case treasury shares, acquired
from earned or capital /paid-in7 surplus, are reissued at
the price for which they were acquired, the result is a
complete restoration of the earned or capital surplus used
in their acquisition."[2] Unfortunately, the apparent con-
viction of this statement is unsupported by legal authority.

The proceeds of the sale of treasury stock are amounts
paid in by security purchasers; the proceeds are in no sense
corporate earnings. It follows that such proceeds should be
considered an increase in paid-in surplus. And this holds
true regardless of whether treasury stock was purchased
"out of" paid-in surplus or "out of" earned surplus. That

[1]Minn., s. 301.15, subd. 3.

[2]Raymond P. Marple, Capital Surplus and Corporate
Net Worth (New York: The Ronald Press Company, 1936),
pp. 72-73.

the purchase of treasury stock reduced the amount of earnings
retained in the business is no reason to consider the proceeds from the sale of a corporation's own stock to be an
increase in the earnings retained in the business. The
California Corporations Code specifically provides that
the amount of the proceeds from the reissue of treasury
shares be attributed to paid-in surplus.[1]

Where state statutes are not so specific, the legal
effect of the reissuance of treasury stock on the accounts
must be said to be uncertain, at best. The question need
not be resolved here; it is sufficient to acknowledge that
the concept of the corporation as a set of legal relations
does not lead to any particular solution. Unless a matter
is settled by legislation or judicial decision, the analysis of the "accountant-lawyer" must be based on factors
other than this underlying corporate concept.

Stock dividends: The term "stock dividend" refers to the
issuance, by a corporation, of additional shares of any
class of its own capital stock to the presently existing
stockholders of the same or a different class of shares
without the receipt of consideration from such shareholders
but accompanied by an increase in the corporation's legal
capital.[2] A "dividend" has been defined as "an appropriation of current or accumulated earnings with the intent

[1]Calif., s. 1714.

[2]American Institute of Accountants, Committee on
Accounting Procedure, "Corporate Accounting for Ordinary
Stock Dividends," Accounting Research Bulletins, No. 11
(September, 1941), p. 99.

to distribute an equivalent amount of enterprise assets
among the stockholders of a particular class on a pro-rata
basis."[1] If this definition of dividend is accepted, the
term "stock dividend" is a misnomer, for no distribution
of enterprise assets is involved.

The Minnesota Business Corporation Act provides that
"stock dividends" may be declared "out of" earned surplus
or paid-in surplus.

> Upon declaration of a dividend payable in shares,
> the amount of surplus from which such dividend is
> declared shall be capitalized; if a dividend is de-
> clared in shares having a par value, the amount of
> surplus so to be capitalized shall equal the aggre-
> gate par value of such shares; if a dividend is de-
> clared in shares without par value, then if such shares
> are preferred shares they shall be capitalized at the
> amount to which such shares, upon involuntary liquida-
> tion, are entitled in preference to shares of another
> class or classes; or, if such shares are common shares
> they shall be capitalized on the basis of the estimated
> fair value of such shares upon allotment as determined
> by the board of directors.[2]

The provisions of the California statute are the same
except that "dividends payable in shares" may also be declared "out of" reduction surplus.[3]

The legal result of the declaration of a "stock
dividend," therefore, is the transfer of a portion of some

---

[1] Paton (ed.), Accountants' Handbook, p. 1039.

[2] Minn., s. 301.22, subd. 3. It is interesting to note
that the Committee on Accounting Procedure of the American
Institute of Accountants has recommended that the amount
of surplus (earned) to be capitalized in conjunction with
a "stock dividend" be determined on the basis of fair value
for all "dividend" shares including those having a par
value. "Restatement and Revision of Accounting Research
Bulletins," Accounting Research Bulletin, No. 43 (1953),
p. 51.

[3] Calif., s. 1504.

kind of surplus to stated capital accompanied by an increase
in the number of shares of stock issued and outstanding.
State statutes generally provide also for a transfer from
earned or paid-in surplus to legal capital upon a resolution of the board of directors <u>without</u> the concurrent issue
of additional shares of stock.[1] In either case, the total
of legal capital plus surplus remains unchanged.

What are the economic effects that should be recorded
in the accounts of a corporation conceived as a social
institution? The total assets of the institution and the
composition of those assets remain unchanged by the declaration and distribution of "stock dividends." There has been
no additional capital derived from stock issues; the source
of the additional <u>legal</u> capital represented by shares of
stock issued as "stock dividends" is existing surplus which
has either already been paid in by stockholders or has been
earned. That is, the increase in <u>legal</u> capital is accomplished by the "capitalization" of accumulated undistributed
earnings or perhaps the "legal capitalization" of amounts
which were derived from stock issues but which were in
excess of certain arbitrarily designated amounts. Undistributed earnings which have not been legally capitalized
may very well be as irrevocably dedicated to the corporate
enterprise as those earnings which have been transferred
to legal capital by means of a so-called stock dividend.

---

[1]"The shareholders or directors may at any time by
resolution transfer amounts from paid-in or earned surplus
to stated capital." <u>Minn.</u>, s. 301.21, subd. 7. See also
<u>Calif.</u>, s. 1903.

From an economic viewpoint, therefore, the accounts
of the incorporated social institution are unaffected by
"stock dividends." Only the descriptive information concerning the number of shares issued and outstanding is
changed. It would perhaps be desirable for some purposes
to indicate in appropriate financial statements, by footnote or otherwise, the amount of legal capital as determined
by someone competent to make the necessary legal analysis.
If economic information is to be provided, however, periodic
and/or cumulative reports of the sources and applications
of funds might be used to indicate the expediency of re-
taining some or all of earnings.

Changes in ownership and owners' obligations, on the
other hand, may result from "stock dividends." Accordingly,
in accounting for an association of individuals, certain
effects must be recorded.

A "dividend" of preferred stock to either preferred
shareholders or common shareholders increases the association's obligation to preferred security holders. A common
shareholder receiving a preferred "dividend" has, in
effect, relinquished part of his ownership in favor of a
senior security. A transfer from the proprietorship accounts
to the preferred stock account in the amount of the par or
stated value of such preferred shares is required. The
total investment contributions of common shareholders is
clearly undiminished by such a transaction, but whether
the common shareholders are relinquishing all or part of

their ownership resulting from consideration received in excess of par or stated value of preferred stock, if any, or whether it is accumulated undistributed earnings that is diminished, is not so clear. However, the amount of consideration received in excess of the par or stated value of outstanding preferred stock is clearly reduced where additional preferred stock is issued in the absence of any additional consideration. It is reasonable, therefore, that this account, if any, be eliminated before any deduction is made in the amount of accumulated undistributed earnings constituting proprietorship. It would be possible to account separately for that obligation to preferred shareholders resulting from investment contributions and that resulting from the transfer of claims to accumulated undistributed earnings. Such information, however, is probably not important to common shareholders, the proprietors for whose information the accounts are presumably maintained.

If common shares are distributed as "stock dividends" to either preferred shareholders or common shareholders, there is no change in common shareholders' total proprietorship. The composition of that proprietorship is likewise unchanged. There have been no additional investment contributions by common shareholders and the amount of undistributed earnings is unchanged albeit part of that amount may no longer be legally distributable. What has already been said about the usefulness of supplementary

information with regard to legal capital and with regard
to the retention of earnings applies equally well to this
concept. Although here the accountant is primarily concerned
with accounting for proprietorship, which is to some extent
a legal concept, the analysis of transactions should be
primarily from an economic rather than legal viewpoint.

The effects of "stock dividends" upon the common
shareholders' equity in a separate and distinct entity are
identical to the effects upon tne proprietorship of an
association of individuals; the effects upon the preferred
shareholders' equity are the same as those previously
described upon the association of co-owners' obligations
to preferred stockholders. The corporation may be read-
justing the equities between common and preferred shareholders or merely changing the legal form of the common
shareholders' equity. In any event, there are no new
investment contributions to account for.

It is recognized that the analysis of "stock dividend"
transactions proposed here as being consistent with the
association of individuals concept and the concept of
separate and distinct entity is somewhat unorthodox.
Typically, the procedures suggested in accounting textbooks
and other accounting literature call for a transfer from
accumulated undistributed earnings to the relevant capital
stock account. Henceforth the balances of capital stock
accounts are a mixture of shareholders' investment
contributions and earnings "plowed back" into the

business.[1] If separate accounts are maintained for paid-in
surplus items, a transfer from accumulated undistributed
earnings to such accounts may also be advocated. The
balances of such accounts then defy classification. They,
too, become a mixture of shareholders' investment contributions and undistributed earnings and, from a legal viewpoint, a mixture of paid-in surplus and earned surplus.
There is no legal provision or justification for redesig-
nating earned surplus as paid-in surplus.[2] Such a designation would undoubtedly have no legal effect.

These procedures are sometimes rationalized by
analogizing the issue of "stock dividends" with a simul-
taneous payment of a cash dividend and sale of stock to
the recipient for the same amount. Determination of acceptable accounting procedures via the process of analogy is
expedient where there is no better basis. The analogy in
this case is not acceptable because it is quite unnecessary.
The legal or economic facts are clear and the effects of
"stock dividend" transactions, if any, should be reflected
in the accounts accordingly. Furthermore, the analogy is
lacking; in the case of a "stock dividend" the recipient
has had no choice of alternative investments, he has not
decided how little or how much to invest--in fact, he has
not made a decision to invest at all. It is misleading

---

[1]This "mixture" may indicate the legal capital,
however.

[2]See Minn., s. 301.22, subd. 3, quoted on p. 118,
supra.

to imply that earnings "capitalized" by means of "stock dividends" constitute additional shareholders' investment contributions. "Capitalization" of earnings by this means merely changes the legal restrictions pertaining to that portion of undistributed earnings. The analysis of transactions may be legal or economic but, where there is contradiction, confusion of the two approaches leads to no useful result.

That other types of confusion may arise in connection with "stock dividends" is exemplified by the recommendation of the American Institute of Accountants. This is doubly unfortunate, for the Institute's pronouncements carry a not insignificant weight of authority in the public accounting profession. Although it is acknowledged that "stock dividends" are not really dividends at all, the accounting procedure advocated is based on the recipient's assumed misconception to the contrary.

> . . . A stock dividend does not, in fact, give rise to any change whatsoever in either the corporation's assets or its respective shareholders' proportionate interests therein. However, it cannot fail to be recognized that, merely as a consequence of the expressed purpose of the transaction and its characterization as a dividend in related notices to shareholders and the public at large, many recipients of stock dividends look upon them as distributions of corporate earnings and usually in an amount equivalent to the fair value of the additional shares received. Furthermore, it is to be presumed that such views of recipients are materially strengthened in those instances, which are by far the most numerous, where the issuances are so small in comparison with the shares previously outstanding that they do not have any apparent effect upon the share market price and, consequently, the market value of the shares previously held remains substantially unchanged. The committee

therefore believes that where these circumstances
exist the corporation should in the public interest
account for the transaction by transferring from
earned surplus to the category of permanent capitalization (represented by the capital stock and capital
surplus accounts) an amount equal to the fair value
of the additional shares issued. Unless this is done,
the amount of earnings which the shareholder may believe to have been distributed to him will be left,
except to the extent otherwise dictated by legal requirements, in earned surplus subject to possible
further similar stock issuances or cash distributions.[1]

The tendency of the recommended procedure is clearly

to mislead further the naive recipient of the "stock dividend"

rather than attempt to convey to him the proper significance

of the transaction. The notion of "permanent capitalization"

is also questionable. It implies that any remaining balance

of undistributed earnings is retained only temporarily and

that subsequently assets are to be distributed in this

amount. Actually "stock dividends" are more likely to be

distributed for their effects on market quotations or their

placating effects on the recipient shareholders than in an

attempt to designate "permanent capitalization." Since

legal provisions generally exist for the reduction in the

amount of legal capital, even that amount cannot neces-

sarily be considered "permanent."[2]

Stock splitups: The term "stock splitup" refers to the

division of issued shares into a greater number of shares

of the same class without change in the aggregate amount

---

[1]A.I.A., "Restatement," op. cit., pp. 51-52.

[2]An interesting but largely unrelated controversy
is concerned with the question whether "stock dividends"
constitute income to the recipient.

of legal capital.[1] A stock splitup of common shares differs
from a stock "dividend" of common shares to common shareholders <u>only</u> in that an increase in <u>legal</u> capital accompanies
the stock "dividend" whereas no change in <u>legal</u> capital is
involved in a stock splitup. Presumably, the chief purpose
of a splitup of the shares of a corporation is "to reduce
the market value of the shares so that they may obtain a
wider distribution."[2]

The <u>Minnesota Business Corporations Act</u> provides

---

[1]Minn., s. 301.22, subd. 4; Calif., s. 1507; Paton
(ed.), <u>Accountants' Handbook</u>, pp. 1014-1015; Vatter,
"Corporate Stock Equities," <u>op. cit.</u>, p. 390; A.I.A.,
"Corporate Accounting for Ordinary Stock Dividends," <u>op.
cit.</u>, p. 99.

It is to be noted that, in 1953, the Committee on
Accounting Procedure of the American Institute of Accountants
adopted a new and unique definition of the term "stock
splitup": "An issuance by a corporation of its own common
shares to its common shareholders without consideration
and under conditions indicating that such action is prompted
mainly by a desire to increase the number of outstanding
shares for the purpose of effecting a reduction in their
unit market price and, thereby, of obtaining wider distribution and improved marketability of the shares."

According to this new definition, the issuance of
additional shares to the extent of more than "say, 20%
or 25% of the previously outstanding shares" constitutes
a "stock splitup" because of the effect on market values
even though a capitalization of surplus accompanies the
issue. It is proposed that the classification of a transaction as a "stock dividend" or "stock splitup" be determined by whether the transaction "has, or may <u>reasonably
be expected</u> to have, the effect of <u>materially reducing</u>
the share market value." A.I.A., "Restatement," <u>op. cit.</u>,
pp. 49 ff. (italics mine). Henceforth, what may be a
"stock dividend" to one accountant may be a "stock
splitup" to another.

[2]Dewing, <u>op. cit.</u>, II, 1185 ff.

for such "split or subdivision of shares"[1] but, because
only the number of shares issued and outstanding is changed,
there is nothing to be recorded in the accounts in order
to reflect the notion of the corporation as a set of legal
relations. There is likewise no effect upon the accounts
of the association of individuals, the separate and distinct entity, or the social institution; there are no
resultant changes in proprietorship, equities, or sources
of capital, respectively. It is believed that accountants
are in complete agreement on this point.

Conversion of capital stock: Preferred shares are sometimes convertible into common shares at the option of the
preferred shareholders. Other capital stock conversion
arrangements are also possible but somewhat less likely
to be found. From the legal point of view the conversion
of preferred shares to common shares results in a decrease
in the legal capital represented by the par or stated
values of the converted preferred shares and an increase
in the legal capital represented by the par or stated
values of common shares. If the decrease in legal capital
exceeds the increase, paid-in surplus arises in the amount
of the excess. A legal capitalization of earned surplus
would result should the increase in legal capital represented by common shares exceed the decrease represented
by preferred shares.

Assuming no receipt or distribution of assets in

---

[1] Minn., s. 301.22, subd. 4.

connection with the conversion, it is appropriate that the
source of the pertinent portion of capital of the incorporated economic institution be redesignated. The original
classification of investment contributions received in
consideration for convertible preferred shares is a tenta-
tive one. The act of converting constitutes an irrevocable
determination as to the class of investment and reclassifi-
cation in the accounts is required. A pro rata share of
the capital tentatively classified as being derived from
preferred stock issues becomes capital derived from common
stock issues. Since there is no distribution or acquisition of assets, it would be erroneous to change the balance
of accumulated undistributed earnings or other capital
source in connection with such a conversion.

Conversion of stock constitutes an adjustment among
the equities of the separate and distinct entity; the equity
of preferred shareholders is reduced and the equity of common shareholders is increased. The magnitude of the adjustment will ordinarily be the par or stated value of the
retired preferred shares. A pro rata portion of the account
containing consideration received in excess of par or stated
value of preferred stock should likewise be transferred to
the investment contributions of common shareholders. In
any event, there is no change in the amount of accumulated
undistributed earnings.

Preferred obligees of the association of common
shareholders become members of the proprietary group upon

conversion. The change should be reflected in the association's accounts in exactly the same manner as in the accounts of the separate and distinct entity. Pro rata transfers from the account containing the par or stated values of preferred shares and the account containing excess consideration should be carried to the account containing investment contributions of common shareholders. There is no change in the amount of accumulated undistributed earnings because there is no loss or gain to the common shareholders on the transaction. It was known at the outset that the original consideration was received for either a specified number of preferred shares or a specified number of common shares, which one to be determined later as changes in their relative market values developed.

Bond Transactions

Issuance of bonds: "Bonds are essentially long term corporate notes issued under a formal legal procedure and secured either by the pledge of specific properties or revenues or by the general credit of the issuer. The typical bond contract calls for a series of 'interest' payments semiannually and payment of principal or face amount at maturity."[1] These securities differ from stocks principally because of the contractual nature of the promise to make specified payments on specific

---

[1]Paton (ed.), Accountants' Handbook, p. 938.

dates.[1] The market value of a bond is therefore equal
to the present value of the amount due at maturity plus
the present value of the series of semiannual "interest"
payments, both determined at the appropriate yield rate
of interest.

In accounting, the difference between the market value
at the date of issue and the maturity or "face value" is
commonly referred to as bond premium or bond discount.
Although such premiums or discounts have no legal or economic significance, customarily bond issues are recorded
as an increase in an asset account in the amount of the
proceeds, an increase in the bond account in the amount of
the maturity value, and an increase in a bond premium or
bond discount account in the amount of the difference between proceeds and maturity value.[2] The account for bond
premium or discount is a valuation account and must be
considered to be inseparably related to the bond account
containing the maturity value. For example:

```
Bonds, 20-year, 4% debentures, due 1970   $1,000,000
Less:  Unamortized bond discount              50,000
       Book value of bonds outstanding      $ 950,000
```

or

```
Bonds, 20-year, 6% debentures, due 1970   $1,000,000
Plus:  Unamortized bond premium               50,000
       Book value of bonds outstanding      $1,050,000
```

---

[1]Income or revenue bonds represent a partial exception to this statement. The periodic "interest" payments
on such bonds are contingent upon the earning of net income
or revenue as defined in the bond contract. The payment
at maturity, however, is not contingent.

[2]The costs of issuing the bonds will be ignored on
the grounds such costs are not germane to this discussion.

Unfortunately, unamortized bond discount and unamortized bond premium are seldom disclosed in the manner
illustrated. Conventional accounting practice favors the
classification of unamortized bond discount among the assets
as a "deferred charge," presumably on the grounds that it
represents a kind of long-term prepayment of bond interest.
Unamortized bond premium is generally shown among the liabilities as an item distinct from the maturity value of
bonds, frequently classified as a "deferred credit" in the
same manner as income which has been received in advance.[1]
Such disclosures are consistent with the definitions of
"asset" and "liability" which were proposed by the Committee
on Terminology of the American Institute of Accountants in
1941.[2] But, the Committee issued slightly altered definitions in 1953 which explicitly exclude from "assets" what

---

[1]Published annual reports are often not in great
enough detail to disclose these items specifically, but
the results of the examination by the A.I.A. of the annual
reports published by 600 industrial companies support the
general statements made above. A.I.A., Accounting Trends
and Techniques in Published Corporate Annual Reports (8th
ed.; New York: American Institute of Accountants, 1954),
pp. 88-90 and pp. 105-107.

[2]"Asset: A thing represented by a debit balance
(other than a deficit) that is or would be properly carried
forward upon a closing of books of account kept by double-
entry methods, according to the rules or principles of
accounting." "Liability: A thing represented by a credit
balance that is or would be properly carried forward upon
a closing of books of account kept by double-entry methods,
according to the rules or principles of accounting, provided such credit balance is not in effect a negative balance applicable to an asset." A.I.A., Committee on
Accounting Procedure, "Report of Committee on Terminology,"
Accounting Research Bulletins, No. 9 (Special) (May, 1941),
pp. 82-83.

is "in effect a negative balance applicable to a liability."
However, with respect to "deferred charge," the 1953 committee declares that "it is not an asset in the popular
sense, but if it may be carried forward as a proper charge
against future income, then in an accounting sense, and
particularly in a balance-sheet classification, it is an
asset."[1] As long as practicing accountants look upon unamortized bond discount as a deferred charge, therefore, it will
continue to be shown among the assets.

The legal aspects of bond transactions are largely
governed by the law of contracts and, in some instances,
by the law of negotiable instruments. The concept of the
corporation as a set of legal relations, therefore, is
satisfied by the recording of the contractual obligation
in the proper amount. The present value of the future
contractual payments, based on the yield rate, seems most
appropriate. The total of cash payments to be made would
overstate the current value of the obligation and the amount
of that overstatement would not be represented by anything
that could reasonably be considered an asset.

Outstanding bonds are an obligation of the owners
of the corporation conceived as an association of individuals. The obligation must be recorded in the appropriate
amount in an account properly designated for such obligations, such as Long-term Debt.

---

[1]A.I.A., Committee on Terminology, "Review and
Resume," Accounting Terminology Bulletins, No. 1 (1953),
p. 13.

Bondholders have an equity in the separate and distinct corporate entity which, except for the particular
terms of the contract, is similar to the equities of stockholders. Bondholders, as well as stockholders, have invested
in the corporate entity and have acquired certain rights
(equities) as a result of their investment. The amount
of the bondholders' equity resulting from a corporation's
bond issue is identical to the amount of the debt of an
association of individuals arising from a like issue. The
account of the corporate entity to be increased as a result
of a bond issue is properly described as "bondholders'
equity."

As a social institution, the issuance of bonds merely
represents another source of corporate capital. The transaction results in an increase in assets, usually cash, and
an increase in capital derived from outstanding bond issues,
both increases being measured by the amount of the proceeds.
It is reiterated, bond premium and bond discount have no
legal or economic significance and a separate account for
such amounts is not required by any of these concepts of
the corporation.

Retirement of bonds at an amount less than book value: If
sufficient cash is available, the issuer may find it desirable to reacquire outstanding bonds by purchasing them on
the market prior to maturity. And if yield rates of interest
or other significant factors have changed in the market
since the date of issue, the market value of the bonds

will presumably be more than or less than book value.[1]
Assuming market value to be lower than book value, the difference between the amount of the decrease in assets and the
amount of the decrease in debt resulting from such reacqui-
sitions by an association of individuals represents an
increase in ownership.

The economic events and influences which permit this
kind of an increment to ownership are difficult if not
impossible to identify. In the simplest case the gain is
a windfall brought about by the exogenous increase in yield
rates of interest. Investors' opinions with respect to the
financial soundness of the corporate obligor and other equally
nebulous influences may also cause declines in market values.
The increment to ownership is obviously not related to the
owners' investment contributions and because other types
of windfall gains and losses ultimately are reflected in
the accumulated undistributed earnings account, that account
will not be corrupted by including "earnings" resulting from
the financial operations of the association.

To the separate and distinct corporate entity there
is no gain on the transaction. Total equities remain
unchanged; the difference between the bondholders' equity
and the cash payment merely represents a transfer to the
common shareholders' equity because theirs is residual in
nature. If the usefulness justifies the cost of accumulating

---

[1]As used here, book value is the current value of the
contractual payments as determined at the rate of interest
which the bonds were originally issued to yield.

such information, a separate account may be maintained for
each unique component of the common shareholders' equity.
In any event, this increment to the common shareholders'
equity can in no sense be properly described as accumulated
undistributed earnings. That account is intended for increases in common shareholders' equity resulting from the
earnings of the corporation, the separate and distinct
entity for which the accounts are constructed. In this
case, the corporate entity has earned nothing. To consider
that account a record of accumulated undistributed earnings
of the common shareholders would be essentially to adopt
the concept of the corporation as an association of individuals. The nature of the increment is an adjustment among
equities not unlike the equity adjustment occasioned by the
receipt of consideration in excess of par or stated value
of preferred stock. The amount is properly described as
excess of book value of bonds over cost of retirement.

It must be acknowledged that Paton and Littleton,
who advocate corporate accounting based on the concept of
separate and distinct entity, do not entirely agree with
the preceding analysis.

> The calling of outstanding bonds, for example, is
> a transaction which affects the arrangements with those
> who supply the capital of the business; it is quite
> distinct from the stream of operating activity and
> attendant utilization of resources. It might seem to
> follow, then, that a gain from such a transaction should
> be reported as a capital adjustment, a credit repre-
> senting a nominal donation by one group of investors
> to another class of investors. There are difficulties,
> however, in the way of the adoption of this view. The
> distinction between bondholders (representing creditor-

136

capital) and stockholders (representing residual-
capital) is of marked importance from the legal standpoint and hence must be given serious recognition in
financial administration and accounting. Thus the
redemption of a bond at less than recorded value involves
something more than a realignment of the total stock
equity; there is an actual increase in the total acknowledged amount of such equity without any further contribution by the shareholder. In the light of these
considerations the increase in the stock equity realized
upon the retirement of a liability at less than book
value is generally treated as income and is so regarded
in Federal tax administration.[1]

It is submitted that the Paton and Littleton treatment

is not consistent with the concept of separate and distinct

corporate entity. The corporation as something separate and

distinct from bondholders and stockholders cannot create

income merely via equity adjustments. Interestingly, this

contention is supported by Paton, writing alone, in the

revised edition of Essentials of Accounting.

    Granting that the precise effect of eliminating
debt by paying substantially less than the face or book
amount may be debatable, it seems clear that the balancing credit does not represent actual revenue and
cannot reasonably be viewed as reflecting taxable
income. If treatment as a general valuation offset
to assets is not considered practicable it is still
desirable to exclude such items from earnings and report
them as a special adjustment of the stock equity.[2]

This represents a change of view on the part of Paton, for

in the first edition of Essentials of Accounting he refers

to the excess of the book value of debt over the cost of

retirement as "Profit on Bond Retirement."[3]

_____

[1]Paton and Littleton, op. cit., pp. 116-117.

[2]Paton, Essentials of Accounting (Revised ed.; 1949),
p. 770.

[3]Paton, Essentials of Accounting (1938), p. 732.

From the legal point of view, the difference between the book value of bonds, a liability, and the cost of retirement accrues to the benefit of the stockholders. It clearly does not constitute an increase in legal capital and therefore it necessarily represents an increase in surplus. It cannot be said with equal confidence, however, whether the increase in surplus has been "paid in" or "earned." In Minnesota, for instance, these classifications of surplus are quite inadequately defined:

> . . . The excess of . . . /fair/ value /of the assets of a corporation/, if any, above the aggregate of the liabilities and stated capital of the corporation shall constitute the aggregate of its paid-in and earned surplus, and the balance remaining, if any, after deducting therefrom the earned surplus of the corporation, shall constitute its paid-in surplus.[1]

But although various transactions which give rise to paid-in surplus are enumerated, nowhere is earned surplus defined. Nor is it clear that paid-in surplus arises only from the transactions specifically enumerated.

The same is true of the California statute. Stated capital is defined and specific transactions giving rise to paid-in surplus and reduction surplus are enumerated. It must be inferred that all unspecified increments to surplus are earned.

Presumably, the law of corporations is concerned with the protection of the rights of creditors, preferred shareholders, and common shareholders in that order. As far as creditors are concerned, it makes no difference which

---

[1] Minn., s. 301.22, subd. 1.

surplus account is increased; the real question is whether
this "gain" on the retirement of bonds should increase the
surplus available for dividends to preferred shareholders
only, i.e., paid-in surplus, or increase the surplus available for dividends to both common and preferred shareholders,
i.e., earned surplus. There seems to be no reason why the
strength of the position of preferred shareholders before
the bond retirement transaction would be adversely affected
by considering the "gain" from retirement an increment to
earned surplus. And paid-in surplus thereby continues to
be derived solely from amounts paid in by stockholders.

Conceived as a social institution, any capital derived
from corporate bond issues which is not withdrawn at the
time of the retirement of those bonds constitutes a kind
of involuntary "contribution" left with the institution.
It seems more appropriate that the amount be considered an
addition to the contributed or invested capital of the
institution rather than considered corporate earnings and
accordingly it should be adequately described so as to
indicate its source. "Capital contributions derived from
retired bond issues" is perhaps acceptable.
Retirement of bonds at an amount greater than book value:
Bonds may also be retired prior to maturity under circumstances which require payments to be made which exceed
their book values. The retirement of bonds issued by the
incorporated social institution constitutes the withdrawal
of capital supplied by a particular class of investors.

If the amount of assets given in retirement exceeds the
book value of that investment, a distribution of accumulated
earnings is made.

The retirement of the debt of the incorporated association of individuals at a cost in excess of the book value
of that debt produces a loss which diminishes the common
shareholders' proprietorship. This loss represents a reduction in accumulated undistributed earnings, if any, or an
increase in the association's deficit.

The separate and distinct corporate entity suffers
no loss from the retirement of bondholders' investment, but
rather distributes a "bonus" portion of accumulated earnings
to the retiring equityholders. This generous act of the
corporate entity is apparently made at the expense of the
common shareholders whose equity is reduced accordingly.
Presumably, however, such premature retirements result in
future benefits to the corporation which will ultimately
accrue to the common shareholders' equity and more than
offset the seeming current detriment.

This type of transaction has no effect upon the legal
capital of the corporation concerned. And, because it
could be construed as having an adverse effect on the preferred shareholders' liquidation position,[1] the excess of
retirement payment over book value undoubtedly represents
a decrease in earned surplus rather than paid-in surplus.

---

[1]Amounts paid in excess of the maturity value of bonds
represent decreases in assets which would otherwise be available to satisfy the claims of preferred shareholders.

<u>Conversion of bonds to capital stock</u>: In order to make
bonds more marketable, or for other reasons, bond contracts
sometimes provide for conversion to capital stock at the
option of the bondholder. The analysis of the conversion
transaction may be made from either of two points of view.
The cancellation of the bonds may be considered to be the
consideration received for the stock issued, or the stock
issued may be considered the consideration given in retirement of the bonds. It has been suggested that this distinction is significant in determining the <u>amount</u> of the
consideration; the consideration <u>received</u> for the stock
issue is the book value of the bonds while the consideration
<u>given</u> for the bond redemption is the market value of the
stock.[1]

It would seem that market quotations are the better
measure of value for either the bonds or the stock and that
at the time of any conversion the market values should be
equal. When the bonds are first issued, the conversion
price specified in the bond contract is inevitably greater
than the market value of the stock. The market value of
the bonds at the time of issue then is the present value
of the "interest" and maturity payments based on an appropriate yield rate of interest. The market value of the
bonds will continue to be so based until the market value
of the stock exceeds the conversion price. Thereafter

[1]Wilbert E. Karrenbrock and Harry Simons, <u>Intermediate
Accounting, Standard Volume</u> (2d ed.; Cincinnati, South-
western Publishing Company, 1954), pp. 406-407.

the bonds will be valued according to the shares of stock
for which they may be exchanged.

Bonds which are purchased and sold when the market
value of stock is greater than the specified conversion
price are not traded as bonds but rather as claims to a
specified number of shares of stock. In effect, the market
"converts" the bonds when the market price and conversion
price of stock become equal. Theoretically, if there has
been no change in the yield rate of interest to the time the
market makes such "conversion," the market value of the bonds,
the market value of the stock, and the book value of the
bonds will all be equal. Any lapse of time between the time
the market "converts" the bonds and the time the administrative formalities of issuing stock certificates and can-
celing bond certificates take place might well be ignored
for valuation purposes. The conversion price is the fair
market value of the stock at the time the conversion effectively takes place.

The relevant consequence of this line of reasoning
is that the book value of the bonds is the appropriate
measure of consideration regardless of whether the transaction be viewed primarily as a stock issue or primarily
as a bond retirement. The underlying concept of the corporation does not affect that measurement unless something
to the contrary be specified in corporate statutes, in which
case the legal view must prevail in order to manifest the
concept of the corporation as a set of legal relations.

The consideration having been determined, the issuance of capital stock should be analyzed as discussed at the beginning of this chapter and, because there is no "gain or loss" on the bond retirement, the bond accounts should simply be eliminated.

CHAPTER VI

THE EFFECT OF THE CONCEPT OF THE CORPORATION
ON THE ACCOUNTING FOR THE MEASUREMENT AND
DISTRIBUTION OF CORPORATE INCOME

Introduction

In order to discuss the effects of the four concepts
of the corporation on the accounting for the measurement
and distribution of income, it is essential that the concept of corporate income contemplated be clearly established.

A meaningful and useful concept of income is apt to
be quite independent of the concept of the corporation or
even the legal form of business organization. On the other
hand, given an acceptable definition of income, the concept
of the corporation might well dictate the classification of
certain transactions as transactions which affect its
measurement or transactions which constitute its distribution.

It is well outside the scope of this study to advocate
and defend a particular income concept. Rather, the definition of income which is adopted will be based on what
seems to be the consequence of current generally accepted
accounting practices. Whether or not such an income concept
is desirable or useful is irrelevant to this study.

Income: Basically, income is an economic concept. One
lucid exposition of the economic notion of income is that

of J. R. Hicks:

> The purpose of income calculations in practical
> affairs is to give people an indication of the amount
> which they can consume without impoverishing themselves.
> Following out this idea, it would seem that we ought
> to define a man's income as the maximum value which
> he can consume during a week, and still expect to be
> as well off at the end of the week as he was at the
> beginning. Thus when a person saves, he plans to be
> better off in the future; when he lives beyond his
> income, he plans to be worse off. Remembering that
> the practical purpose of income is to serve as a guide
> for prudent conduct, I think it is fairly clear that
> this is what the central meaning must be.[1]

The measurement of how "well off" an individual or
business unit is implies the determination in real terms of
the capitalized value of prospective receipts. The uncertainty of prospective receipts and the uncertainty with
respect to price levels and relevant interest rates have
thus far prevented practicing accountants' measuring
income in that sense. To a great extent, accountants have
ignored price levels, interest rates, and future prospects
and have accepted invested cost in terms of numbers of
dollars as an appropriate valuation. For the most part,
at the date of acquisition invested cost is the market
value and presumably market value represents the best
estimate of the capitalized value of prospective receipts
(of cash or valuable services). Subsequent changes in out-
look, the value of the dollars invested, and the relevant
rate of interest are ignored for accounting purposes.

Accordingly, for the purposes of this study, Hicks'
definition of income is modified to define corporate

<u>income</u> during any given period of time as the maximum amount,
expressed in dollars, which, if there were no additional
investments during the period, could be distributed by the
corporation to its beneficiaries without impairing the
cumulative dollar amount of cash or other assets which
were invested in the corporation at the beginning of the
period.[1]

The concept of the corporation dictates those who are
properly deemed to be corporate "beneficiaries." The common
shareholders are the beneficiaries of the corporation conceived as an association of co-owners; according to the
"entity theory" of accounting, all equityholders are the
beneficiaries of the separate and distinct corporate entity;
the entire populace is the beneficiary of the social institution; and all owners of shares of stock, preferred as well
as common, are looked upon as corporate beneficiaries from
a legal viewpoint.

The concept of the corporation likewise determines
"the cumulative dollar amount of cash or other assets" which
may properly be considered to constitute <u>investment</u> at the
beginning of the period in contrast to obligations or debt.
In the association of common shareholders, typically, the
investment at the beginning of the period would consist
of the original common shareholders' investment contributions and any accumulated undistributed earnings. According

---

[1]For a comprehensive discussion of concepts of business income see Charles E. Johnson, "The Concept and Measurement of Business Income for Corporate Reporting" (Unpublished
Ph.D. dissertation, University of Minnesota, 1952).

to the notion referred to as that of a separate and distinct
entity, investment includes the equities of bondholders
(perhaps also other types of long-term creditors), preferred shareholders, and common shareholders. From a legal
viewpoint, the total of legal capital, paid-in surplus, and
earned surplus, constitutes investment. In the case of the
corporation conceived as a social institution, all sources
of corporate capital (assets) represent investment in the
enterprise.

Revenues and gains: In accounting, corporate income is
measured by the excess of the amount of "revenues" and
"gains" over the amount of "expenses" and "losses" during
a given period of time. Unfortunately, no acceptable concept embracing both "revenues" and "gains" is to be found
in the accounting literature and even the separate terms
"revenues" and "gains" seem to have no single precise
meanings.

A useful concept of revenue seems to call for something similar to Irving Fisher's concept of "gross income,"
i.e., "the value of all services flowing from an article
of wealth through any period."[1] Such a concept of revenue
lends economic and managerial significance to its measurement.

Using Fisher's concept as a point of departure, for
the purposes of this study corporate revenue is defined as
the flow of funds (acquisition of assets or diminution of

[1]Irving Fisher, The Nature of Capital and Income
(New York: The Macmillan Company, 1906), p. 121.

debt, expressed in dollars) into the corporation as a result
of the furnishing of goods or services.[1] Goods is meant
to be interpreted as the tangible product of the enterprise
and services is meant to include those services provided
by the use of corporate assets as well as personal services.
Services, therefore, embraces the use of corporation cash
as in the case of a loan granted by the corporation or an
investment made by the corporation and the use of corporation buildings or equipment as in the case of rentals.

Revenues, however, are not the only source of corporate
income. In this study, income increments resulting from
transactions other than revenue transactions will be identified as gains. Admittedly, gains, so defined, does not
represent a singularly significant concept--the term covers
a variety of heterogeneous transactions. This is inescapable
because of the nature of the practical limitations inherent
in the accounting process of determining corporate income.

So-called capital gains make up the greatest share
of the income increments which fall into the gains classification. But, in a sense, even capital gains constitute
a heterogeneous group of transactions. In general, the
excesses of proceeds received upon the sales or exchanges
of assets, other than the products or stock in trade, over
the book values of such assets are considered to be capital

[1]"Flow concepts" of revenue are advocated by Paton
and Littleton, op. cit., p. 47; Finney and Miller, op. cit.,
p. 596; and commented upon by Perry Mason and Sidney
Davidson in Fundamentals of Accounting (3d ed.; Brooklyn:
The Foundation Press, Inc., 1953), pp. 149-150.

gains.[1] Such gains, however, may actually constitute a
correction of prior years' depreciation estimates or they
may reflect a higher price level, or a lower interest rate
as well as improved expectations. In any case, capital
gains are income increments within the scope of the concept
of corporate income found in current accounting practice
and adopted for this study. Except for their income-aug-
menting effect, gains have little in common with revenues.

Expenses and losses: Expenses are defined here as those
costs which are identified with particular streams of current revenues as distinct from those costs which will normally
be identified with future streams of revenues. Costs which
cannot logically be identified with any revenue, either
past, present, or future, are losses.[2]

Costs, such as salesmen's commissions and the costs
of goods sold, may be identified directly with particular
revenues. Costs may also be identified with particular
revenues indirectly because they represent costs incurred
in the general operations of the business during a particular

[1]Paton (ed.), Accountants' Handbook, p. 162. The
definition of capital assets for federal income tax purposes
excludes also real or depreciable property used in the trade
or business (Internal Revenue Code of 1954, s. 1221) but
provides that, where gains on such assets exceed losses,
the gains shall be treated as capital gains (s. 1231).

[2]This definition of expense represents only a slight
modification of the concept suggested by Robert B. Bangs
in "The Definition and Measurement of Income," The Accounting
Review, XV (September, 1940), pp. 360-361. A similar notion
of expense is expressed by Paton in Essentials of Accounting
(Revised ed.), p. 82: "Expense may . . . be defined as the
cost of the volume of revenue arising in the particular
period."

revenue period.

Summary: In accounting, periodic corporate income is measured by aggregating the corporate revenues (the flow of
funds into the corporation as a result of furnishing goods
or services) and gains during a period of time and deducting
therefrom the corporation's expenses (costs identified with
that period's revenues) and losses during the same period.
The difference, assuming a successful period, represents
corporate income (the number of dollars which could have
been distributed to corporate beneficiaries during that
period without impairing the cumulative dollar investment).

Interest Charges

The magnitude of interest charges on short-term obligations is apt to be relatively insignificant and immaterial.
Our attention, therefore, will be directed primarily to an
examination of the effects of concepts of the corporation
on the accounting for the interest charges on long-term
securities, such as bonds. The same line of reasoning,
however, can be applied to the interest charges on short-
term obligations.

To the incorporated association of common shareholders,
bonds represent a liability or debt of the corporation.
Interest charges on that debt are a financial expense--
the interest charges of a given revenue period represent
a cost of financing the general operations of the corporation during that period. Common shareholders are looked

upon as the beneficial owners and interest charges must be
deducted from revenues and gains in measuring the number
of dollars which the corporation could distribute to the
common shareholders without impairing their cumulative
investment.

On the other hand, in measuring the income of the
corporation conceived as a separate and distinct entity
existing and operating for the benefit of all equityholders,
interest charges are not an expense. The proceeds of bond
issues represent the investment and measure the equity of
the owners of those bonds. Interest payments made by the
corporation to bondholders constitute the distribution of
their contractual share of corporate income. In the words
of Paton and Littleton,

> To management the bondholders' dollars and the money
> furnished by the stockholders become amalgamated in the
> body of resources subject to administration, and the
> net income of the enterprise consists of the entire
> amount available for apportionment among all classes
> of investors. Interest charges, from this standpoint,
> are not operating costs but represent a distribution
> of income, somewhat akin to dividends.[1]

In Accounting Theory, Paton reasoned, "There is no
fundamental antithesis between payments to the stockholder
(dividends) and return to the bondholders (interest). Both
represent distributions of income."[2]

It is to be noted, however, that this view may lead
to perplexing results. What is the nature of interest payments made to bondholders during a period in which corporate

---

[1] Paton and Littleton, op. cit., pp. 43-44.

[2] Paton, Accounting Theory, p. 267.

151

income is inadequate or in which corporate losses have
occurred? If any undistributed earnings have accumulated,
such interest payments may still be looked upon as distributions of income earned in prior periods; but, if there
are no accumulated undistributed earnings, clearly interest
payments cannot constitute income distributions. From
the so-called entity point of view, interest payments made
under these circumstances must be looked upon as a return
or withdrawal of investment. But it cannot be a return
of the bondholders' investment because their investment
equity is not reduced by these payments; it is the investment equity of the common shareholders which is diminished.
It seems somewhat illogical to treat such interest payments
as a withdrawal of investment when the equityholders'
investment withdrawn is that of the common shareholders
and the equityholders receiving the withdrawal are bondholders. Under these conditions is it not difficult to
consider the common shareholders and the bondholders as
being members of a single equityholding group having common
interests in the corporation?

From the viewpoint of law, interest charges are
expenses which are deducted in the process of income measurement. Corporate bonds are looked upon as liabilities or
debt, and bond interest charges are deductible in determining
the incomes of corporations for federal income tax purposes.[1]
It is generally accepted that where corporate statutes

[1] Internal Revenue Code of 1954, s. 163.

refer to a corporation's income, as in the case of provisions for legal payment of dividends "out of its net earnings for its current or for the preceding fiscal year,"[1] interest charges represent deductions in the income measuring process.

Interest charges represent a valid economic cost of the use of the capital supplied by bondholders to the incorporated social institution. In determining the dollar amount which could have been distributed to society, perhaps in the form of lower prices or improved product, without impairing the cumulative number of dollars invested in the corporate institution, interest charges must be deducted on an equal footing with wages and rents.

Income Taxes

In general, property taxes, payroll taxes, and other taxes whose amounts are independent of the results of operations create no special problems--they are accepted as expenses or production costs, whichever is applicable. On the other hand, perhaps because of the contingent nature of their occurrence and magnitude, the treatment of income taxes is less standardized.

To those advocating the concept of the corporation as an association of individuals, income taxes are clearly an expense. Their contingent nature does not alter the necessity of deducting income taxes from revenues and

[1]Minn., s. 301.22, subd. 2(3). See Calif., s. 1500(b) for similar provisions.

gains in measuring the amount which could be distributed
to the common shareholders without impairing their cumulative investment. This view is in agreement with that of
the Committee on Accounting Procedure of the American
Institute of Accountants: "Income taxes are an expense
that should be allocated, when necessary and practicable,
to income and other accounts, as other expenses are
allocated."[1]

A consistent application of the corporate concept
underlying the entity theory of accounting leads to the
same conclusion. In measuring the income of a corporation,
income taxes must be deducted. The state and federal governments are not generally deemed to be corporate investors.
Accordingly, the number of dollars which could be distributed
to corporation equityholders without impairing their cumulative investment is clearly adversely affected by the imposition of income taxes. According to Paton,

> Taxes are a somewhat anomalous element in business
> finance. Taxes are coerced; their amount is largely
> outside the control of management; they do not follow
> price trends closely; they can hardly be said to mea-
> sure the value of services received and utilized in
> production. Taxes, therefore, are not strictly con-
> gruous with ordinary expenses. However, taxes are
> clearly a deduction from or charge against revenues
> in the process of determining net income.[2]

In accordance with the definitions used in this study,
income taxes are expenses indirectly identified with the
revenues of the separate and distinct corporate entity as

---

[1] A.I.A., "Restatement," op. cit., p. 38.

[2] Paton, Essentials of Accounting (Revised ed.), p. 99.

an unavoidable cost of general business operations during
a given revenue period.

If the assertion is accepted that from the legal viewpoint the stockholder group, preferred shareholders as well
as common shareholders, are looked upon as corporation
beneficiaries, income taxes must also be treated as expenses
in the determination of the income of the corporation.
There is little doubt that when the Minnesota statute cited
earlier refers to "net earnings," earnings net of income
taxes, among other things, is intended. In line with the
definition of income utilized in this study, the periodic
amount distributable to all classes of shareholders without
impairment of their cumulative investment is determined
after the deduction of income taxes.

Presumably, the members of society are beneficiaries
of the social institution. Ideally then, corporation operations should be designed to furnish desirable products at
cost (including a fair return to suppliers of capital), in
which case there would be no corporate income (economic
profit). This is approximately the goal of the various
state and federal agencies which have been charged with
the responsibility of regulating the operations of companies
in the field of public utilities.

As an alternative to direct regulation, the imposition
of income taxes might be looked upon as a method of siphoning
off a substantial portion of corporate income to finance
the services provided by the several levels of government

to the ultimate benefit of society. This kind of rationale is particularly applicable to the form of taxation known as "excess profits taxes" which was imposed during both World Wars and the Korean conflict. Marginal tax rates as high as 85.5 per cent have been justified on the basis of the social repugnancy of profits created by bloodshed.

From this point of view, income taxes might well be treated as a distribution of corporate income to members of society, the corporate beneficiaries, through the medium of governmental agencies. This necessarily assumes that the incidence of the corporation income tax falls upon the incorporated institution; that the tax is not shifted forward in the form of higher prices for the corporation's product or shifted backward in the form of lower prices for the factors of production. Otherwise, the corporation income tax is not an effective siphon of economic profits.

It would be difficult, however, to rationalize as distributions of corporate economic profits the other kinds of taxes which are imposed upon the corporation. Their payment is independent of the existence of such profits. Some taxes represent, in a sense, payments for services received by the corporation itself. For example, gasoline taxes are, in a general way, related to the use made of the system of highways. Property taxes, at least to some extent, defray the costs of fire protection, police protection, and general maintenance of the streets and sewers utilized by tax-paying corporations. Even if their

incidence should be upon the corporation, payroll taxes
are clearly a direct cost of the services of labor. And,
it is generally acknowledged that, although paid by the
corporation, commodity taxes are frequently shifted to
customers and/or resource owners.[1]

The view that income taxes represent the distribution
of income has been advocated by some on grounds which seem
to be unrelated to any concept of the corporation. For
instance, the following paragraph is found in Mason's and
Davidson's Fundamentals of Accounting:

> To the stockholders income taxes are as much of
> an expense as property taxes, and it clearly is erroneous
> to use the net income before deducting income taxes as
> an indication of the benefit which stockholders receive
> from the operations of a corporation. At the same time,
> there is much to be said in support of the treatment
> of the provision for income taxes as a distribution
> rather than a determinant of net income. If there is
> no net income, there is no income tax. From the mana-
> gerial viewpoint, the net income before deducting
> interest and income taxes is a more meaningful indica-
> tion of the results of operations and one which can more

---

[1]"Even though taxes on commodities are usually collected from the sellers of taxed commodities, it is generally
believed that such taxes are shifted--that the economic
unit from which the tax money is collected does not bear
all of the tax and that relative commodity and resource
prices are altered as a result." O. H. Brownlee and
Edward D. Allen, Economics of Public Finance (2d ed.;
New York: Prentice-Hall, Inc., 1954), p. 286.

"The consumption taxes, including excises, tariffs,
special and general sales taxes (possibly also gross income
taxes), are regarded as the most easily shifted of all
taxes. Indeed, they are called consumption taxes not
because they are levied upon the consumer--the impact is
usually on the merchant or manufacturer--but because it
is thought that he will bear the ultimate burden."
Harold M. Groves, Financing Government (4th ed.; New
York: Henry Holt and Company, 1954), p. 136.

effectively be compared from one period to another.
We shall, therefore, treat income taxes as a share
of the Federal and, in some cases, state governments
in the net income of a corporation--an income distribution rather than an expense.[1]

The dependency of the existence and magnitude of
income taxes upon the existence and magnitude of taxable
income is, of course, inherent in the particular method
used in measuring the amount of the tax. Certain bonus
arrangements for management personnel are also frequently
dependent upon the results of operations in much the same
manner. The measurement of "wage payments" to employees
in that fashion, however, has apparently not affected their
acceptance as expenses. It is likewise true that if there
is no real property, there is no real property tax, and
the amount of real property tax depends directly on the
amount of real property. A corporation which rents rather
than owns real property pays no real property tax as such.
Does that mean that should the corporation acquire real
property, the property taxes imposed on the acquisition
constitute a distribution of income rather than an expense?

As for the managerial viewpoint, there can be no
doubt that tax planning represents an extremely significant factor in modern decision-making on the part of corporation managements. This would seem to indicate that
management's primary concern is the amount of profits
after taxes rather than the amount before taxes.

The argument that "net income before deducting

[1]Mason and Davidson, op. cit., p. 168.

interest and income taxes is a more meaningful indication
of the results of operations" for comparing "one period
to another" is generally raised in favor of segregating
revenues and expenses into operating and nonoperating
classifications. Operating revenues are those revenues
derived from the primary source of revenues (e.g., sales)
and operating expenses are the costs identified with the
attainment of those revenues. The difference between
operating revenues and operating expenses constitutes
operating income (or loss). Operating income, therefore,
is not affected by the magnitude of nonrecurring gains
and losses, incidental revenues and expenses, or the capital structure of the corporation.

Clearly, those nonoperating items which must be
deducted from revenues and gains in the measurement of
corporation income are determined by the concept of income
and the concept of the corporation. It is believed that
the concept of income adopted for this comparative study
of the effects of different concepts of the corporation on
accounting is reasonably representative of the popular
notion of business income. Other factors, such as the
contingent nature of deductions and the comparability of
the resultant incomes of different periods, are irrelevant.

Dividends

In keeping with the definition of dividends suggested
in Chapter VI in connection with the discussion of so-called

stock dividends, the term "dividends" is restricted here
to pro rata distributions of corporate assets to shareholders made in connection with current or accumulated
earnings. In the very large majority of cases dividends
are distributed in the form of cash, but the possibility
of distributions of other forms of assets does not alter
the basic analysis of the dividend transaction.

From the point of view of those who look upon the
corporation as an association of common shareholders,
dividends to preferred shareholders represent an expense
akin to interest charges. Such dividends represent payments for the use of the capital supplied by the original
purchasers of preferred shares. The amount which could be
distributed to common shareholders without impairing their
cumulative investment is determined only after allowing for
preferred dividends whether actually paid or, in the case
of cumulative preferred stock, merely accrued. This treatment is manifested in the typical computation of the period's
earnings per share of common stock or the computation of
the book value of common shares. In the words of Husband,

> The preferred stockholders occupy a "hybrid" position,
> a resultant of the cross breeding of bonds and common
> stock. On the theory that the common stockholders
> occupy the entrepreneurship position in the corpora-
> tion, preferred stock, like bonds, represents the
> hiring of capital service. Consistent therewith pre-
> ferred stock dividends are best treated as a cost.[1]

Dividend payments made to common shareholders represent distributions of corporation income to the co-owners
of the corporation. The amount which could be distributed

---

[1]Husband, "The Entity Concept in Accounting," op. cit.,
p. 561.

to association members (common shareholders) as dividends
without impairing their cumulative investment is the corporation's income. The difference between the amount of
income and the amount which is distributed as dividends
constitutes undistributed income which may be allowed to
accumulate for use in the business.

The concept of the corporation as a social institution also requires the treatment of dividends on preferred
stock as an expense. Such dividends represent payments for
the use of the capital supplied to the corporation by the
original purchasers of preferred shares. Accordingly,
dividend payments to preferred shareholders are expenses
to the incorporated social institution and, if cumulative,
should be accrued in the accounting records in the absence
of actual disbursement.

But dividends on common stock are also an expense to
the incorporated social institution. The original purchasers of common shares supply capital to the corporation;
dividends represent payments for its use. Bonds, preferred
stock, and common stock all represent sources of corporate
capital and, in general, the rates of return on these three
types of investments may be expected to vary with the degree
and nature of the risks involved.

From a strictly legal viewpoint, dividends on both
preferred stock and common stock constitute a distribution
of corporation income. Preferred shareholders, as well
as common shareholders, are considered corporation

beneficiaries and the benefits of successful corporate operations are distributed to both groups in the form of dividends. Dividends are not deductible in the determination of taxable income, and it is equally clear in state corporation statutes that periodic corporate income ("net earnings") is to be measured before allowing for dividend payments to any class of stockholders.

The separate and distinct corporate entity existing and operating for the benefit of all suppliers of corporate capital likewise distributes the benefits accruing to preferred and common shareholders through the medium of dividend payments. Interest payments to bondholders, dividend payments to preferred shareholders, and dividend payments to common shareholders must be looked upon as shares in the success of corporate operations rather than compensation paid by the corporation for the use of their capital.

CHAPTER VII

THE EFFECT OF THE CONCEPT OF THE CORPORATION
ON THE ACCOUNTING FOR OTHER CHANGES
IN THE ACCOUNTS RELATED TO THE
INTERESTS OF CORPORATE
SECURITY HOLDERS

Introduction

There are certain other transactions for which we
might expect the accounting analysis to be affected by
concepts of the corporation. Four types of such transactions will be considered in this chapter with the objective
of establishing a pattern of analysis which could be applied
to still other transactions should these four not exhaust
the possibilities. The transactions to be examined are
donations, appreciation, appropriations of accumulated
undistributed earnings, and business combinations.

Donations

Donations refer to the acquisition of assets, the
cancellation of obligations, or the acquisition of outstanding shares of stock without consideration passing from
the corporation to the donor. Historically, donations of
outstanding shares of stock have been viewed with suspicion
as acts designed to circumvent any contingent liability in
connection with the issuance of par value stock at an amount
less than par value.

According to Finney and Miller:

Stock is sometimes issued to the organizers of a corporation for non-cash assets and a portion of the stock is
then donated to the company to be resold to provide
working capital. This procedure was often used by mining
and other speculative companies before the introduction
of no-par stock made the expedient unnecessary. If such
a company undertook to sell par value stock to the public, the stock usually had to be offered at a discount
to make it attractive. But if unissued stock were sold
at a discount, the purchasers would be liable for the
discount, and the discount liability might detract from
the salability of the stock. Such companies therefore
resorted to the "treasury stock subterfuge." By issuing all of the stock for the mine or other property
and reacquiring part of it as treasury stock, the reacquired stock became, theoretically at least, fully paid
treasury stock which could be resold at a discount.[1]

In 1912, the State of New York passed legislation
which permitted the use of shares without par value and "by
1928 the corporation law of practically every state in the
Union permitted the issue of no-par stock for at least some
types of corporations."[2] Then, beginning in the 1920's,
shares of stock with a very low or nominal par began to be
used as a means of minimizing state taxes which are levied
on par values and treat no-par stock as having a par value
of $100.[3] The present-day widespread use of no-par and
low-par stock has obviated the "treasury stock subterfuge."
In the discussion which follows, therefore, it is assumed
that all donations are made and received in good faith.
Donations of outstanding shares: From the viewpoint of
an association of common shareholders, the accounts of the
corporation are not affected by the donation of common shares.

---

[1]Finney and Miller, op. cit., p. 290.
[2]Dewing, op. cit., I, 59.   [3]Ibid., pp. 66-67.

The number of shares issued and outstanding is reduced but
the total investment contributions of common shareholders
remains unchanged. The effect of such a donation is to
increase the value of the remaining common shareholders'
interests in the corporation and accordingly benefit them
individually rather than as an association.

The donation of preferred shares represents the gratuitous forgiveness of an association obligation. Total
proprietorship is thereby increased in the amount of the
book value of the canceled obligation. The book value of
the acquired preferred shares should be transferred to an
appropriate proprietorship account. This addition to proprietorship has not been _earned_ in any meaningful sense
and therefore does not constitute an increase in the amount
of accumulated undistributed _earnings_. The nature of the
increase is not unlike that of premiums received upon the
original issue of preferred shares and perhaps a single
account for proprietorship increments derived from preferred
stock transactions is appropriate.

The effects on the corporation's accounts of the
reissue of donated shares, like the effects of the reissue
of purchased treasury shares, are indistinguishable from
the effects of the issuance of previously unissued shares.[1]

The notion of a separate legal entity existing for
the benefit of all equityholders requires analyses of transactions involving the donation of stock identical to that

---

[1]The issuance of capital stock is discussed in
chap. v, _supra_.

above. The donation of common shares does not change the equity of common shareholders as a group; the donation of preferred shares operates to transfer a pro rata portion of preferred shareholders' equity to the equity of common shareholders; and the effect of reissuing donated stock is identical to the effect of original stock issues and the reissuance of purchased treasury shares.

Legal capital is not affected directly by the act of donating outstanding shares to the corporation. It does, however, facilitate a subsequent reduction in the amount of legal capital by the prescribed legal procedure.[1] But until some independent legal action is taken with respect to donated shares there are no changes to be recorded in the accounts of the corporation viewed solely as a legal body. The Minnesota statutes do not deal with donated shares explicitly. It seems reasonable, however, that the retirement or reissue of donated shares be treated like the retirement or reissue of treasury shares which have been purchased or redeemed. The California Corporations Code specifically provides that donated shares "may be carried as treasury shares or may (at the option of the board of directors) be retired."[2]

The donation of outstanding shares of either preferred or common stock to the social institution has no effect on the assets which have been made available for corporate

___

[1] See Retirement of treasury stock, chap. v, supra.
[2] Calif., s. 1709.

operations. The original sources of corporate assets are likewise unaffected. It does, however, relieve the corporation from the obligation of making payments (dividend distributions) for the use of the capital provided at the time of the original issue of the donated shares. For this reason it would seem appropriate that the amount of capital derived from the issuance of stock which has been gratuitously returned to the corporation be segregated from the amount of capital associated with outstanding shares for which the corporation is obliged, where feasible, to make use payments. A capital source, perhaps called **donations**, might be designated which would include capital originally derived from the issue of stock but with respect to which all claims have been relinquished and which is therefore effectively donated.

Any distinctions between authorized and unissued shares, purchased or redeemed treasury shares, and donated treasury shares are purely legal. From an economic point of view, all shares of a particular class of stock in the hands of the issuing corporation are homogeneous. Accordingly, when shares are issued by the incorporated social institution, the analysis of the transaction is not affected by capricious designations on the part of corporate officials that the issue is made from shares previously unissued, or from treasury shares for which consideration was given, or from donated treasury shares. The economic analysis is not affected by that kind of arbitrary manipulation.

Gratuitous forgiveness of obligations: Much that has
already been said with respect to the donation of outstanding shares is applicable to the forgiveness of obligations.
For instance, the donation of preferred shares to the association of individuals is analogous to the forgiveness of
other kinds of obligations commonly referred to as liabilities or debt. Forgivenesses of these types result in aug-
mentations of proprietorship which can hardly be considered
to have been earned. An appropriately descriptive designation of the source of proprietorship should be made. "Forgiveness of debt" is explicit.

A transfer from the donor's equity to the residual
equity of common shareholders must be made in keeping with
the entity theory of accounting. Except for terminology,
the effect on the corporation's accounts is identical to
that consistent with the proprietary theory.

Where the pertinent state statutes do not specify
the legal effects of gratuitous cancellations of liabilities,
the concept of the corporation as merely a set of legal
relations is sterile as a basis for accounting analysis.
The forgiveness undoubtedly operates to increase surplus,
but whether in the eyes of the law such surplus is paid-in
or earned depends upon judicial interpretation. It would
seem that the protection of other creditors and preferred
shareholders would not be endangered to any greater degree
by making the amount of the donation available for distribution to common shareholders (earned surplus) than it

would by the routine payment of the obligation. However,
should it be deemed desirable that donations be treated
so as to improve the position of preferred shareholders,
the resultant surplus increment should be made a part of
paid-in surplus.

If the corporation is looked upon as a social institution, the obligations represented by bonds or notes have
a great deal in common with the obligations represented by
shares of stock. The gratuitous cancellation of obligations
of all these types requires the transfer from a capital
source account representing an obligation of the institution to an obligation-free capital source account. "Donations"
was previously suggested as an appropriate description of
this obligation-free source of capital.

Donations of assets: It is not uncommon that, as a means
of attracting desirable firms and industries, communities
have made land and other assets available without charge.
These donations may be made contingent upon the meeting of
certain requirements such as the employment of a prescribed
minimum number of workers or the occupation and use of the
donated premises for a prescribed minimum number of years.
But, even if conditional, donations of this kind increase
the assets available for corporate operations and accordingly
merit an accounting. The circumstances may not be unlike
the utilization of assets for which legal title will not
be acquired until settlement of a ten or twenty-year mort-
gage note. Of course, donations of assets may be received

from stockholders as well as outsiders. It is generally
agreed among accountants that, while in a sense donated
assets are cost-free, their acquisition should be recorded
at fair market value.

The increase in the assets of the association of common shareholders as a result of donations represents an
increase in proprietorship. The source of this proprietorship is properly described as "donations" as in the case
of forgiveness of debt. From the point of view of the
association these two kinds of donations have the same effect--
the significant result being an increase in the amount of
proprietorship.

From the viewpoint of the corporation as a separate
entity, presumably all equityholders benefit from the donation of assets through the resultant augmentation of properties with which corporate operations may be conducted. This
over-all benefit, however, is not reflected in the accounts--
as in the proprietary theory, it is the common shareholders'
equity alone which is increased. Again, "donations" seems
to describe adequately the nature of this portion of common shareholders' equity.

There is no legal distinction between the forgiveness
of debt and the donation of assets. In the absence of specific statutory provisions or legal precedent, the accountant
advocating the concept of the corporation as a set of legal
relations faces the dilemma of choosing between paid-in
surplus and earned surplus. This is well illustrated in

Capital Surplus and Corporate Net Worth, where Marple
attempts to solve the problem by distinguishing donations
from stockholders, donations of "permanent capital" from
outsiders, and donations by outsiders of capital "available for current use."

> . . . All contributions of stockholders are contribu-
> tions of capital and, to the extent that they do not
> add to legal or stated capital, represent capital
> surplus.[1]
> Turning now to consideration of contributions of
> outsiders there seems to be some doubt as to whether
> such gifts should be classified as contributed capital
> or earned capital. . . . Where the donor intends that
> the gift shall become a part of the permanent capital
> of the corporation, it should be treated as capital
> surplus. Where the gift is not intended as permanent
> capital, but is made available for current use it should
> be treated as earned surplus.[2]

These distinctions are supported in part by the following line of reasoning:

> No one is hurt by the declaration of a dividend from
> a surplus donated for current purposes. Creditors are
> not injured because they have no right to depend upon
> such surplus for the payment of their claims. Neither
> are stockholders injured, because the distribution is
> not made from a surplus contributed by them, but one
> contributed by an outsider. In other words, the capi-
> tal contributed by the stockholders is not being re-
> turned to them.[3]

An illustration which Marple implies is an example
of a donation for current purposes is the donation of funds
to a corporation in temporary financial difficulty in order
that it might meet its payroll.[4]

---

[1]This statement seems to contradict his earlier statement that contributions received for the reissuance of
treasury shares restore earned surplus "used in their
acquisition." See p. 116, *supra*.

[2]Marple, *op. cit.*, pp. 136-137.

[3]*Ibid.*, p. 137. [4]*Ibid.*, pp. 135-136.

These distinctions seem to be made on rather flimsy
grounds. One does not donate surplus but rather donates
assets, and donated assets cannot be both distributed as
dividends and used by the corporation, even in current
operations. If there is an earned surplus, any donation
of assets to a corporation, regardless of the intention or
status (stockholder or outsider) of the donor, affects the
feasibility of dividends or other asset distributions to
shareholders to precisely the same degree. Creditors "have
no right to depend upon" any surplus for the payment of
their claims. Creditors' claims must be paid with assets
and asset distributions to shareholders are limited only
by the amount of legal capital--legal capital being unaffected
by donations. Furthermore, it is not at all clear how stockholders can be "injured" more or less by the receipt of a
distribution of assets donated by an outsider with one set
of intentions, or an outsider with a different set of intentions, or a stockholder whose objectives are apparently
irrelevant. The nature of any distributions of assets which
do not consitute the distribution of corporate earnings
should be clearly designated lest they be misleading.
Finally, the fundamental weakness of analyzing the effects
of donations on the basis of Marple's distinctions is
exemplified by the quandary with which the accountant would
be faced in the event of an anonymous donation.

Donations of assets are a source of capital for the
social institution with respect to which there is no obligation on the part of the corporation to make use payments.

From this point of view there is no significant distinction
between the effects of the donation of outstanding shares,
the forgiveness of other kinds of obligations, and the
donation of assets. Assuming there is a market for the
corporation's stock, each of these kinds of donations
increases the availability of assets for general corporate
operations without increasing corporate obligations.

Appreciation

Appreciation has been defined by Paton and Littleton
as "the excess of the estimated 'fair market value' of mer-
chandise, securities, land, buildings, or other property
over the cost of such property or the unabsorbed book balance of depreciable or amortizable elements."[1] Marple suggests three possible explanations for this kind of divergency
between fair market values and book values: past accounting
errors, unearned increments, and a decline in the purchasing
power of money. Unearned increments refer to increases in
fair market value due, not to the overt efforts of the corporation, but to exogenous social or economic influences.[2]

As a general rule, appreciation is not recognized in
corporation accounts until it has been realized by means
of a sale or exchange transaction. It is argued that only
when the value of an asset has been tested by the consumma-
tion of an arm's-length transaction can the amount of

[1]Paton and Littleton, op. cit., p. 62.
[2]Marple, op. cit., pp. 113-117.

appreciation be reasonably determined. It is feared that
fluctuations in value and errors in estimation prior to
realization are apt to create misleading results and that
the acceptance of appreciation estimates might also introduce manipulative opportunities to the unscrupulous. There
are, however, notable exceptions to the general rule. Investment companies frequently report the amount of unrealized
appreciation of securities during the fiscal period as an
adjunct to income and report the fair market value of securities held as an integral part of the balance sheet. The
yearly survey of the annual reports of 600 industrial corporations conducted by the research department of the
American Institute of Accountants also discloses an occa-
sional recognition of appreciation.[1]

No general statement concerning the legal status of
appreciation can be made. In Minnesota, unrealized appreciation of "securities having a readily ascertainable market
value" may be recognized for dividend purposes but not other
"unrealized appreciation of assets."[2] In California, dividends may not be declared "out of the mere appreciation in
the value of its assets not yet realized, nor from earned
surplus representing profits derived from an exchange of
assets unless and until such profits have been realized or
unless the assets received are currently realizable in
cash."[3]

---

[1]A.I.A., Accounting Trends and Techniques, pp. 73 ff.
[2]Minn., s. 301.22, subd. 1.   [3]Calif., s. 1502.

If one is accounting and reporting for the corporation viewed solely as a set of legal relations, therefore, unrealized appreciation of marketable securities only may be recorded in Minnesota, and no unrealized appreciation of any kind merits recording in California. Where unrealized appreciation is recognized, presumably it augments earned surplus--clearly it is surplus and it has not been paid in.

From other points of view, whether or not unrealized appreciation should be recorded and reported would seem to depend upon whether or not the resultant information is more useful. There is nothing inherent in the association of individuals concept, the concept of separate and distinct entity, or the concept of a corporate social institution which precludes the recognition of appreciation. The question at hand, rather, is what are the effects of its recognition, assuming appreciation is to be recognized.

The obligations of the incorporated association of common shareholders to creditors, bondholders, and preferred shareholders are specified in terms of numbers of dollars, whatever their purchasing power. The appreciation in the dollar value of corporate assets does not affect the amount or nature of these obligations and accordingly such appreciation constitutes an increase in the corporate proprietorship.

Appreciation which has been realized by a sales or exchange transaction is reflected in the corporation's earnings. No attempt is made to separate appreciation of inventory items from the value added by the distribution

function of the retailer or the conversion function of the
manufacturer. Appreciation, if any, is included in the
price received at the time of the sale and recorded as
revenue. Appreciation of depreciable assets finds its way
into earnings either by means of a depreciation charge based
on original cost or as a "gain" when a depreciable asset is
sold for a price in excess of book value. No attempt is
ordinarily made to determine whether a "gain" on the disposal of a depreciable asset represents an unearned increment, a correction of prior periods' depreciation estimates,
or appreciation merely in terms of less valuable dollars.
The "gain" is considered income and is reflected in corporate earnings.

Consistent with this practice, it would seem acceptable that unrealized appreciation, if recognized, likewise
be considered income and be reflected in corporate earnings.
The concept of income adopted in the preceding chapter does
not require realization. A more important limitation on
the acceptability of appreciation as an element of income
is the feasibility of objective measurement. The increase
in market value of securities listed with a reputable stock
exchange may be measured accurately and objectively. The
recognition of appreciation of other assets which have
readily determinable market values may likewise be acceptable. For many assets, however, an objective and reasonably
accurate determination of market value is impractical.
Rather than maintain the accounts in terms of subjective

values and introduce possible manipulation of financial
reports, the measurement of appreciation of assets of the
latter type must be postponed until objective measurement
is feasible--probably until realization. This, however, is
a practical matter, not a matter of principle.

The portion of earnings, reported in terms of numbers
of dollars, which may be distributed as dividends to the
common shareholders without contracting corporate operations
is a matter of managerial discretion. Typically, in this
respect, allowance has been made for expansion. This is
not to deny that there may be some informative advantages
in reporting the amount of accumulated undistributed earnings
represented by unrealized appreciation and in that way indicating its nonavailability for dividend distributions. But
to consider realized appreciation available for dividends
as income and unrealized appreciation unavailable as capital, as some suggest,[1] seems irreconcilable.

If appreciation, whether realized or not, is accepted
as a kind of augmentation of dollar income, where identifiable at all it should clearly be identified as being of
a nonoperating nature. The amount of appreciation and
manner of accounting for it are not altered by those concepts of the corporation which are not based solely on the
law. Appreciation increases the number of dollars of common shareholders' equity in accordance with the "entity

_____

[1]See American Institute of Accountants, Committee on
Accounting Procedure, "Depreciation on Appreciation,"
Accounting Research Bulletins, No. 5 (April, 1940), pp. 37-47,
and A.I.A., "Restatement," op. cit., p. 73.

theory" and constitutes a source of additional dollars of
capital for the social institution.

Appropriations of Accumulated
Undistributed Earnings

Portions of accumulated undistributed earnings are
sometimes appropriated to evidence compliance with certain
legal provisions or contractual obligations or for other
purposes prescribed by resolution of the board of directors.
Earnings appropriations of a legal or contractual nature
manifest a restriction upon the amount of dividends which
may be legally distributed by the corporation. Appropriations which are initiated by board resolution do not represent an enforceable restriction upon dividend distributions
but rather imply the voluntary retention of earnings for
specified purposes.[1] Appropriations do not reduce the
amount of accumulated undistributed earnings; they serve
merely to earmark portions of it.

Where the accounts are constructed so as to reflect
primarily a legal point of view, statutory and contractual
restrictions on the amount of earned surplus available for
dividends should be recorded. The legal concept of the
corporation has been interpreted to require the classification of stockholders' interests into three basic categories:

[1]"Temporary" appropriations are referred to here
rather than appropriations which have "permanent" legal
effects as in the case of "stock dividends" or the transfer
of earned surplus to legal capital without an increase in
the number of shares of stock outstanding.

legal capital, paid-in surplus, and earned surplus.[1] These
classifications are entirely legal in nature; they are in
no way based on economic concepts. This kind of information
can only be enhanced by further recordations of enforceable
restrictions upon reductions in the amount of earned surplus.[2] Appropriations for expansion, contingencies, etc.,
are designated by the board of directors primarily for
informational purposes and have little legal significance.
The appropriation can be reversed as easily as dividends
can be declared. Such appropriations may but need not be
reflected in accounting records which are basically designed
to reflect the legal status of the corporation.

The association of individuals concept has been interpreted here to require an accounting for corporate assets,
corporate obligations, and sources of proprietorship. That
part of proprietorship resulting from the accumulation of
undistributed earnings is not affected by statute, contract,
or board resolution. A reasonably lucid explanation or
demonstration by management of the need and wisdom of retention of earnings is praiseworthy, but the mere appropriation
of portions of retained earnings is apt to be unconvincing

---

[1]Certain state statutes may provide for other categories, e.g., in California provision is also made for
reduction surplus.

[2]For a group of "characteristic situations" involving
statutory or contractual restrictions on dividend distributions, see U. S. Securities and Exchange Commission,
Accounting Series Releases (Washington: United States
Government Printing Office, 1948), p. 88.

and inadequate.[1]

These remarks apply equally well to the corporation
viewed as a separate and distinct entity operating in
behalf of all equityholders or the corporation looked upon
as a social institution. In either case, accumulated undistributed earnings represents a source of assets the amount
and nature of which is not affected by its availability for
dividend distribution as determined by law or managerial
intent. It is submitted that legal restrictions should be
determined by someone competent to do so and disclosed as
information supplemental to the accounting statements which
should be primarily designed to reveal economic information.
It would seem, too, that the most enlightening and convincing
economic justification for the retention of earnings could
be presented in the form of a statement of the sources and

[1]This may be illustrated by the type of disclosure
frequently made in corporate annual reports of an appropriation for "contingencies." The nature and imminence of the
"contingencies" contemplated are generally left to the
imagination of the reader and, although the practice now
seems to be on the decline, more often than not the appropriation is shown in such a manner as to lead the reader
to believe it no longer constitutes part of the stockholders'
equity. See A.I.A., Accounting Trends and Techniques,
pp. 110-112.

Another point has been made with respect to the in-
adequacy of information disclosed by appropriations of
accumulated undistributed earnings. "Readers of the balance sheet may wonder why, if appropriations have been
made for . . . a variety of purposes, a balance in unap-
propriated retained earnings has been permitted to accumulate. Unless all, or nearly all of the retained earnings
balance is appropriated, there is little gained toward a
clarification of dividend policy by making any appropriations. Any effort to appropriate all of the Retained
Earnings balance is likely to produce such a multitude of
accounts as to lead to confusion." Mason and Davidson,
op. cit., p. 439.

applications of working capital or perhaps, since dividends
are ordinarily distributed in the form of cash, a statement
of sources and uses of cash. And where the balance of net
working capital, or cash, is increased, verbal explanation
is probably warranted.[1]

Business Combinations

The term "business combinations" refers broadly to all
types of transactions whereby the net assets and operations
of two or more corporations are brought together into a
single corporation. Perhaps the simplest form of combination transaction is that of an outright purchase by one
corporation of the assets of another with or without assumption of the vendor corporation's outstanding debt. This
does not introduce any unique accounting problems--the
acquired net assets are recorded at cost, and there is no
effect on the interests of corporate security holders.

Frequently, however, business combinations are effected
by means of transactions for which the accounting analysis
is less clearly established. Combinations by merger or
consolidation are referred to specifically. These transactions are technically distinct in that a merger of corporations takes place when one of the merged legal entities
continues to exist, its name and charter being used by the

---

[1]This view is not without support. "As a means of
explaining what has become of profit funds an interpreta-
tive statement of funds or other appropriate supplementary
form of report is likely to be more satisfactory than formal
division of the surplus account under special 'reserve'
titles." Paton and Littleton, op. cit., p. 108.

combination; a consolidation results in the formation of
a new legal entity to represent the combination, the legal
entities of all the combining corporations ceasing to exist.
These distinctions have some legal significance which will
be indicated in the discussion which follows but from an
economic viewpoint it is quite irrelevant whether Corporation A is merged into Corporation B, or Corporation B is
merged into Corporation A, or Corporation C is formed to
consolidate Corporations A and B. The economic facts and
functions of the combination are unaffected by the choice
of these legal alternatives. Consequently, the term "pooling
of interests" has frequently been used in referring to combinations by merger or consolidation without differentiating
between them.

Perhaps the most difficult problem arises in determining at the outset whether a given combination constitutes
a purchase or a pooling of interests. Various criteria
have been suggested, but it is quite impossible to draw a
well defined line of distinction. The Committee on Accounting
Procedure of the American Institute of Accountants has suggested consideration of the following factors:

> . . . In a pooling of interests, all or substantially
> all of the equity interests in predecessor corporations
> continue, as such, in a surviving corporation which
> may be one of the predecessor corporations, or in a
> new one created for the purpose. In a purchase, on
> the other hand, an important part of all of the owner-
> ship of the acquired corporation is eliminated. A plan
> or firm intention and understanding to retire capital
> stock issued to the owners of one or more of the cor-
> porate parties, or substantial changes in ownership
> occurring immediately before or after the combination,
> would also tend to indicate that the combination is a
> purchase.

Other factors to be taken into consideration in
determining whether a purchase or a pooling of interests is involved are the relative size of the constituent companies and the continuity of management or
power to control the management. Thus, a purchase may
be indicated when one corporate party to a combination
is quite minor in size in relation to the others, or
where the management of one of the corporate parties
to the combination is eliminated or its influence upon
the management of the surviving corporation is very
small. Other things being equal, the presumption that
a pooling of interests is involved would be strengthened
if the activities of the businesses to be combined are
either similar or complementary. No one of these factors would necessarily be determinative, but their
presence or absence would be cumulative in effect.[1]

The Minnesota Business Corporation Act provides that

"two or more corporations . . . may merge into one of the

constituent corporations or consolidate into a new corpora-

tion"[2] and specifies the legal procedure to be followed.

The accounting required to reflect the legal status of the

combination depends entirely upon the technical nature of

the legal procedure chosen. Whatever the choice, it must

be said that, in a pooling of interests, the effects on

legal capital, paid-in surplus, and earned surplus are

clearly outlined. These effects may be demonstrated with

the following data:

---

[1]A.I.A., "Restatement," op. cit., pp. 55-56.

[2]Minn., s. 301.41, subd. 1.

Separate corporations before combination

	Company A	Company B
Outstanding shares	10,000	3,000
Par value per share	$10	$100
Legal capital	$100,000	$300,000
Paid-in surplus	300,000	---
Earned surplus	600,000	300,000
Total	$1,000,000	$600,000
Book value per share	$100	$200

To simplify the illustration, it is assumed that the
market value per share is the same as the book value per
share and that these values, therefore, are to be used as
the basis for distributing shares among the shareholders
of the combining corporations. This, of course, is a matter
of bargaining rather than a matter of law or accounting.

If Company A is merged into Company B, one share of
Company B $100 par value stock will be exchanged for each
two shares of Company A $10 par value stock. Since the
legal capital "of a consolidated or surviving corporation
at the time it begins business shall be at least equal to
the aggregate par value of the shares having par value to
be distributed pursuant to the agreement of consolidation
or merger,"[1] the legal capital of Company B after the merger
is greater than the aggregate legal capital of the two corporations prior to the merger. The increase in aggregate
legal capital constitutes a capitalization of paid-in surplus
and/or earned surplus to the extent of the increase.

On the other hand, if Company B is merged into Company
A, two shares of Company A stock will be issued for each

---

[1]Ibid., s. 301.45, subd. 2.

share of Company B stock; that is, 6,000 $10 par value
shares of Company A stock will be exchanged for the 3,000
$100 par value shares of Company B stock. Upon completion
of such a merger, the legal capital of the surviving Company
A will be less than the aggregate legal capitals of the
separate companies A and B. "If upon a consolidation or
merger the stated /legal/ capital of the consolidated or
surviving corporation shall be less than the aggregate of
the stated capital of the constituent corporations, the
amount of such difference shall constitute paid-in surplus."[1]

The third alternative for pooling interests is the
consolidation of companies A and B into a new Company C.
Should it be deemed desirable to maintain legal capital at
the aggregate of that of Company A and Company B, the
$400,000 could be divided by an appropriate number of shares
to determine a convenient par or stated value for such
shares. The accounts of Company C could then also include
paid-in surplus and earned surplus at the aggregate figures.
"When two or more corporations shall hereafter be consolidated or merged, the earned surpluses of the constituent
or merged corporation or corporations may, to the extent
that they are not capitalized upon such consolidation or
merger, be treated as earned surplus by the consolidated
or surviving corporation."[2]

Upon the accomplishment of the combination under each
of these legal alternatives, the accounts of the combined

---

[1] Ibid., s. 301.21, subd. 5.
[2] Ibid., s. 301.21, subd. 9.

corporation would appear as follows:

Combined corporation after merger or consolidation

	First Alternative Surviving Company B	Second Alternative Surviving Company A	Third Alternative Consolidated Company C
Outstanding shares	8,000	16,000	16,000
Par value per share	$100	$10	$25
Legal capital	$800,000	$160,000	$400,000
Paid-in surplus	---	540,000	300,000
Earned surplus	800,000	900,000	900,000
Total	$1,600,000	$1,600,000	$1,600,000
Book value per share	$200	$100	$100

Should a par or stated value of $100 per share be
designated for the 16,000 shares of Company C stock, the
combination would have $1,600,000 legal capital and no paid-
in or earned surplus. The amounts of the two kinds of surpluses can be determined at will by the designation of the
legal values of the shares of stock.

These results emphasize the fallacy of maintaining
accounts in such a way as to reflect the legal status of
the corporation if it is expected that the resultant information is to be used for any kind of economic analysis. In
a combination, the legal information is apt to vary not
with any changes in economic factors but rather according
to the arbitrary selection of a corporate name (Company B,
Company A, or Company C) and/or the arbitrary designation of
a par or stated value for the shares of stock to be issued.[1]

---

[1]The California Corporations Code does not spell out
the effects of a merger or consolidation as clearly as the
Minnesota statute, but "the surplus appearing on the books
of the constituent corporations, to the extent to which it

Among accountants who are not primarily concerned with
constructing and maintaining accounts to provide information
relative to the corporation's legal status, there are opposing
views with respect to the analysis of transactions resulting
in a pooling of interests. The basic disagreement centers
upon the propriety of considering the accumulated undistributed earnings (earned surplus) of absorbed corporations to
be accumulated undistributed earnings of the absorbing corporation.

The pros and cons are well represented in the accounting
literature, and although it does not always appear explicitly that the proposed analysis relies on a particular
concept of the corporation, the opposing views do appear
implicitly, perhaps even unconsciously, to depend upon underlying corporate concepts This observation is supported,
to some extent at least, by the fact that certain accountants
who advocate a given corporate concept in other instances
take a position with respect to the pooling of interests
which might very well be rationalized on the basis of the
corporate concept they champion.

Proponents of the entity theory of accounting presumably base their analysis of transactions, where it is
relevant, on the concept of the corporation as a separate
and distinct legal entity. This notion precludes the

---

is not capitalized by the issues of shares or otherwise,
may be entered as earned or paid-in surplus, as the case
may be, on the books of the consolidated or surviving corporation" (s. 4117), and, in general, the results of mergers
and consolidations in Minnesota are also obtainable in
California (s. 1709 and ss. 4100 ff.).

possibility of looking upon a business combination as the
pooling of the interests of two groups of equityholders.
The separate and distinct corporate entity may acquire the
net assets of some other corporation, but it remains separate
and distinct from the corporation which disposes of its
assets and the equityholders of that corporation. Perhaps
the most significant and unique consequence of an analysis
of a combination transaction based on the entity concept,
therefore, is the exclusion from the accumulated undistributed
earnings (earned surplus) account of any amount which has
been earned by some other corporate entity. The net assets
received by the surviving or new corporate entity are looked
upon as consideration for its shares issued in exchange.

The results of an accounting analysis based on the
entity concept may be illustrated with the data used to
demonstrate the legal analysis. Assuming the book values
of the net assets acquired are the same as their "fair market value," the $1,000,000 in net assets acquired by Company
B from Company A constitutes an investment contribution in
consideration for the issuance of 5,000 shares of Company
B stock.

Should Company A acquire the $600,000 net assets of
Company B, those assets would be looked upon as an invest-
ment contribution in consideration for the issuance of
6,000 shares of Company A stock. And if a new corporation,
Company C, is formed to acquire the net assets of Companies
A and B, all net assets received from both Company A and
Company B are investment contributions.

The results of the entity concept analysis are summarized as follows:

Combined corporation after merger or consolidation

	First Alternative Surviving Company B	Second Alternative Surviving Company A	Third Alternative Consolidated Company C
Outstanding shares	8,000	16,000	16,000
Par value per share	$100	$10	any amount
Investment contributions	$1,300,000	$1,000,000	$1,600,000
Accumulated undistributed earnings	300,000	600,000	---
Total	$1,600,000	$1,600,000	$1,600,000
Book value per share	$200	$100	$100

These kinds of results have been summarized by Marple as follows:

> . . . In a merger an existing corporation absorbs one or more of the existing companies. Under this type of combination, it is proper for the absorbing corporation to continue to report its accumulated earned surplus, but since the total net worth of the merged corporations is contributed to the continuing corporation for the stock issued, none of the earned surplus of the absorbed companies should be carried over to the new company. . . .
> In the case of a consolidation, a new company is formed to take over the combining corporations. . . . it is not possible for a new corporation to have an earned surplus at its inception. . . .[1]

Similar conclusions have been elaborated upon in the following fashion:

> The element of the total stockholders' equity represented by income retained in the business has significance only to the entity through which the income was produced; it is literally impossible to transfer this factor in any meaningful sense to any other entity. . . .
> The theory that the retained earnings of the disappearing company should be transferred as such to the

[1]Marple, op. cit., pp. 149-150.

189

accounts of the surviving company is a little more
plausible where the acquiring company is a new corporation, organized expressly for the purpose of "taking
over" an existing company, as in this situation the new
concern can be described with some reason as the successor
of the acquired company. Here too, however, the fact
that a new entity has been legally established constitutes an effective roadblock to an assumption that the
identity of the recorded retained earnings of the old
company--or any part thereof--is preserved. The fact
is that the predecessor company has been terminated as
a legal entity and a new concern has emerged, and this
transformation creates a very strong presumption that
a new focus of accountability must be recognized.[1]

Advocates of the proprietary theory of accounting are
primarily concerned with the accounting for the proprietorship of the common shareholders. As long as there is a continuing association of common shareholders, changes in the
name or form of the legal entity by means of which the business of the association is transacted are irrelevant. It
is to be noted that the concept of the corporation as an
association of common shareholders leads to a single set
of accounting information regardless of the legal entity
which survives or succeeds.

For example, this concept may be applied as a basis
for analyzing the combination transactions which have been
used for the preceding illustrations. The accounts of
Company A, Company B, or Company C, immediately after the
combination indicate investment contributions of common
shareholders amounting to $700,000 and accumulated undis-
tributed earnings of $900,000. The $700,000 represents
amounts invested by individual volition in an association
which is still in existence, albeit greatly expanded.

---

[1]Paton and Paton, op. cit., pp. 40-41.

Proprietorship resulting from the accumulation of undistributed earnings, as in contrast to the investment of
individuals, totals $900,000.

The following statements have appeared in support of
the aggregation of the accumulated undistributed earnings
of combining corporations:

> In a true merger, one or more corporations may
> cease to exist as legal entities, but their assets, lia-
> bilities, and earning power continue over into the sur-
> viving corporation, and stockholders of all corporations
> entering into a merger continue to have substantially
> what they had prior to the merger.[1]

> . . . When a combination is a merger the aspects of
> buying and selling are absent and new costs are not
> established. Here, ownerships are pooled but not ter-
> minated, and there is a continuity not present when
> properties are sold. The unique and significant con-
> sequence of this fact is that it is appropriate to
> carry forward into the merger the combined earned sur-
> pluses of the predecessor corporations which are parties
> to it.[2]

> The rationale of the organic merger, . . . rests
> upon the contention that the significant entity is
> not the legal unit used as a convenient vehicle for
> carrying on group activities but rather the actual
> economic or operating unity by means of which the
> owners derive benefits.[3]

The concept of the corporation as a social institution
requires an accounting for an economic enterprise rather
than an accounting for a legal entity, an accounting for
the equities of security holders of a legal entity, or an

---

[1] W. M. Black, "Certain Phases of Merger Accounting,"
The Journal of Accountancy, LXXXIII (March, 1947), p. 215.

[2] Edward B. Wilcox, "Business Combinations: An
Analysis of Mergers, Purchases, and Related Accounting
Procedure," The Journal of Accountancy, LXXXIX (February,
1950), p. 104.

[3] Moonitz and Staehling, op. cit., II, 335.

accounting for the ownership of a particular group of proprietors. Hence, if the combination results in the con-
tinuance of the old businesses performing the same basic
economic functions, though probably on a different scale
as a result of the vertical or horizontal integration of
the previously separate institutions, the accounts of the
combining corporations should be consolidated in much the
same fashion as the accounts of a holding company and its
subsidiaries are consolidated for reporting purposes. The
accounts of the economic enterprise should be constructed
so as to provide information of an economic nature--the
amount and form of capital available for the operation of
its economic functions and the sources of that capital.
The integration of the economic functions of separate enter-
prises does not alter the classification of that amount of
capital derived basically from the issuance of securities
to investors as in contrast to that amount of capital made
available by the accumulation of undistributed earnings.
The analysis of a combination transaction of the incorporated social institution should not be made to vary with
the name chosen for its legal entity.

It has been assumed in the foregoing discussion and
illustrations that market values per share were equal to
book values per share and that fair market values of assets
were equal to book values of assets. These assumptions
are hardly realistic.

The purpose of the first of these assumptions was
merely to obviate a justification of the exchange of shares

in the ratio of two shares of Company A stock to one share
of Company B stock. Any other ratio agreed upon would produce different account balances only if the accounting analysis were strictly legal. The account balances resulting
from analyses based on the association of individuals concept, the concept of separate and distinct entity, or the
social institution concept are unaffected by the ratio of
exchange.

The second assumption, that fair market values of
assets were equal to book values of assets, was made in
order to simplify the fundamental analysis required by each
concept. The far more likely case where fair market values
are not identical with book values calls for additional
comment.

It was noted at the outset of this discussion of business combinations that in the case of an outright purchase
by one corporation of the assets of another, consistent
with the notion of invested cost, the acquired assets are
recorded at cost and there is no effect on the interest of
corporate security holders. In a pooling of interests, however, the question arises whether or not the book values
of assets should be restated to conform with fair market
values. And, more in point, does the answer to this question depend upon an underlying concept of the corporation?

It seems clear from the provisions of state statutes
that a pooling of interests is accepted in law as a continuation of the separate enterprises--paid-in surplus and earned
surplus are carried forward. Accordingly, any restatement

of book values in terms of fair market values would be in
the nature of unrealized appreciation, which, in general,
is not recognized.

From the proprietary point of view, a pooling of interests likewise constitutes a continuation. The association
of common shareholders continues to exist but with a somewhat expanded membership. Therefore, a revaluation is not
required, and yet, as pointed out earlier, there is nothing
inherent in the association of individuals concept which
precludes the recognition of unrealized appreciation. Such
appreciation should be recognized where it can be measured
objectively and where the usefulness of accounting information is improved by its recognition. The bargaining between
those representing the interests of the proprietors of Corporation A and those representing the interests of the proprietors of Corporation B may or may not constitute a basis
for objective measurement. Influences, such as the "value"
of accumulated losses which may be carried forward or backward for corporation income tax purposes, or the relative
strengths of bargaining positions, may invalidate the bargaining process as a means of objective measurement. In
any event, the important problems of valuation cannot be
adequately dealt with here.

This view is in harmony with the statement of the
Committee on Accounting Procedure of the American Institute
of Accountants:

> When a combination is deemed to be a pooling of
> interests, the necessity for a new basis of accountability

does not arise. The carrying amounts of the assets of
the constituent companies, if stated in conformity with
generally accepted accounting principles and appropriately adjusted when deemed necessary to place them on
a uniform basis, should be carried forward; and earned
surpluses of the constituent companies may be carried
forward. However, any adjustment of assets or of surplus which would be in conformity with generally accepted
accounting principles in the absence of a combination
would be equally so if effected in connection with a
pooling of interests.[1]

The same approach is appropriate for the incorporated
social institution where the economic functions of separate
corporations are continued by a single combined institution.
Revaluation is not required, but the bargaining process
leading up to the agreed ratio of exchange of shares may
constitute an objective measurement of values. And if these
new values are utilized in the accounting records the resultant accounting information may have greater significance
than accounting information based on the book values of the
separate corporations.

From the viewpoint of the separate legal entity there
is, in effect, no continuation of dissolved corporate entities. One corporate entity acquires the net assets of
another or others, and all such acquisitions are analogous
to purchases. Accordingly, acquired assets should be recorded at cost--the fair market value of the shares of stock
issued in consideration by the acquiring corporate entity
or, alternatively, the fair market value of the assets
received. The unique result of an analysis based on the
separate entity concept is that it requires the recordation

---

[1]A.I.A., "Restatement," op. cit., p. 56.

of new "costs" for the assets acquired by the new or sur-

viving corporate entity.

This view is supported by Paton and Paton, who illus-

trate a merger of X Co. and Y Co. with X Co. surviving and

make the following comments:

> . . . Failure to record the actual current value of the
> assets acquired by X Co. through the merger transaction
> would violate the general rule that assets acquired by
> any accounting entity should be recorded at cash cost
> if acquired by purchase and at fair market value--the
> equivalent of cash cost--if acquired by the act of in-
> vestment or in any manner not a purchase. . . .
> This leads to the question of the possible restate-
> ment of X Co.'s position at the point of merger in the
> light of the market value of its shares at that time.
> If current values should be recognized in the case of
> the Y Co.--one component--why should such values not
> be recognized in the case of the X Co., the other party
> to the merger? In considering this question it is im-
> portant to bear in mind that under the assumed conditions
> the X Co. actually survives as a distinct corporation;
> it may not be improper to describe the transaction as
> a merger but the literal fact is that X Co. is expand-
> ing through the acquisition of the Y Co. Hence the
> focus of attention in accounting for the "merger" is
> that of the continuing entity, the X Co. And while
> sound accounting requires recognition of additional
> assets and expanding capital on the basis of the cur-
> rent values of the assets acquired there is no compelling
> reason for an appraisal and restatement of all existing
> assets--either up or down--every time new resources are
> received. On the other hand the occasion of a major
> transaction such as a merger, which necessitates a com-
> plete evaluation of all constituent enterprises in
> arriving at equitable terms, may well be an appropri-
> ate point for a fresh start accountingwise, on the
> basis of current values, right across the board.[1]

And, with respect to the consolidation of X Co. and Y Co.

into a new corporation XY Co., Paton and Paton state:

> In this situation a new focus of accounting responsi-
> bility is created, the XY Co., not coinciding in sub-
> stance with either of the old corporations, and hence
> all assets received by the new concern should be recorded
> at their current cash or equivalent value and the capital

---

[1]Paton and Paton, op. cit., pp. 44-45.

of the enterprise is measured by the total of such values, less liabilities assumed.[1]

There is one other view which probably should be mentioned with respect to the aggregation of the accumulated undistributed earnings of constituent corporations upon a pooling of interests. Some accountants have expressed the view that upon the combination of separate corporations a new economic enterprise is formed regardless of the presence or absence of a continuing legal entity. The consequence of this view seems to be that in all poolings of interests, irrespective of their legal classification as merger or consolidation, the entire net assets of the combining corporations represents investment contributions to the resultant economic enterprise.

According to Sunley and Carter:

> Even though there are varying viewpoints and some statutory authorizations to the contrary, the fact is evident that such surplus as arises from the formation of a consolidation or merger is not earned surplus. Those who view it otherwise fail to take into consideration that the new enterprise resulting from the combination may prove to be unprofitable. The mere fact that the separate units prior to consolidation or merger were operated profitably is not conclusive evidence that when combined the new enterprise may not suffer operating losses. In fact, such combined enterprise is a new and untried combination and can have no earned surplus. The only earned surplus possible to the new combination is that which it has earned itself and has not distributed, or reduced in other ways.
>
> This reasoning leads to the conclusion that surplus arising from the act of consolidating or merging is capital or paid-in surplus.[2]

---

[1] Ibid., p. 46.

[2] William T. Sunley and William J. Carter, Corporation Accounting (Revised ed.; New York: The Ronald Press Company, 1944), p. 427.

Werntz is essentially in agreement:

In my opinion, it is not ordinarily sound in the case of a merger or consolidation to carry forward, as earned surplus of the surviving company, the earned surplus of any company whose existence is terminated. Indeed, where the amalgamation in effect brings into existence a new business or economic enterprise, it is to be doubted whether any earned surplus, even that of a corporation which legally "survives," should be carried forward as earned surplus. There would, of course, be no objection to designating the surviving surplus as "Capital surplus--consisting of the earned surplus of consolidated or merged predecessors." Not to take this position would mean that:

(1) A company by, in effect, a purchase of assets can "make a profit," i.e., increase its earned surplus.

(2) The incongruous result is attained of permitting a company to "start out" with an earned surplus. Clearly, if the merged company occupies a substantially different competitive or bargaining position than its several predecessors, there is something incongruous in measuring the success of the new business by the accumulated earnings of the old business.[1]

Ostensibly, at least, these individuals are concerned with an economic entity rather than a legal entity. They refer to "the new enterprise" and the "new business or economic enterprise" and in the case of a merger there is no "new" legal entity. There seems, however, to be serious confusion between legal concepts of surplus and economic concepts of sources of capital. In addition, both of the above statements seem to imply that the existence and magnitude of an earned surplus (i.e., an accumulation of undistributed earnings) are indicative of the success and profitability of an enterprise. According to such a view, a very profitable company which has distributed all of its earnings to its security holders appears less favorably than a much

---

[1] William W. Werntz, "Corporate Consolidations, Reorganizations and Mergers," The New York Certified Public Accountant XV (July, 1945), p. 381.

less profitable firm which retains some or all of its
earnings. Income statements are a far more reliable source
of information with respect to the profitability and success of an enterprise than are balance sheets. Indeed,
there is "something incongruous in measuring the success"
of any business by the amount of its accumulated undistributed earnings. And to classify the aggregate amount of the
net assets of the combining corporations in such a way as
to imply that it represents the amount of original security
holders' investment contributions (i.e., as capital stock,
and paid-in or capital surplus) is indeed misleading.

It has been suggested that it would be desirable to
segregate and earmark undistributed earnings accumulated
before and after accomplishment of a combination in a manner similar to that practiced in connection with quasi-
reorganizations.[1] This kind of disclosure may represent
an acceptable compromise for those who look upon the carrying forward of the accumulated undistributed earnings of
merging or consolidating corporations as undesirable. The
criterion of full disclosure might well be applied here.

For example, on October 1, 1954, the Packard Motor
Car Company and The Studebaker Corporation pooled interests.
At the end of the preceding fiscal year, December 31, 1953,
the Packard Motor Car Company had assets with a book value
of about $136 million; of this amount, more than $43 million

[1] J. Arthur Marvin, "Corporate Consolidations, Reorganizations, and Mergers," The New York Certified Public
Accountant, XV (July, 1945), p. 376.

represented earned surplus. On the same date, December 31,
1953, the book value of the assets of The Studebaker Corporation was nearly $158 million and its earned surplus
totaled almost $88 million. It appears that the same eco-
nomic functions are to be performed by the combination as
were performed by the separate corporations, but it is
anticipated that the combined operations can be conducted
more efficiently. Accordingly, the earned surpluses of
both "old" corporations have been carried forward as earned
surplus of the "new" Studebaker-Packard Corporation.[1]

Henceforth, will users of the financial statements
of Studebaker-Packard Corporation be apt to be misled if
the amounts of undistributed earnings accumulated prior to
combination are not earmarked and segregated from the amount
of earnings (or, as in this case, losses) accumulated subsequent to combination? Or, using a less negative approach,
would the disclosure of amounts of undistributed earnings
accumulated before and after combination be apt to represent useful information?

Separate disclosures would be most apt to be significant where there are accumulated losses following the
combination. As indicated above, the amount of accumulated
undistributed earnings is apt to be of little value in
assessing the profitability of the corporation without additional knowledge of the amounts of earnings which have been

---

[1]The financial data is based on information contained
in Moody's Manual of Investments, American and Foreign,
Industrial Securities, Vols. 1954 and 1955.

distributed. Disclosures of undistributed earnings accumulated after the date of combination, nevertheless, would
indicate that the combination has not offset losses of the
combination against earnings of the separate corporations
prior to combination and in that limited sense, at least,
such disclosure may be significant.

CHAPTER VIII

SUMMARY AND CONCLUSIONS

This study was undertaken (1) to determine what concepts of the corporation have been recognized as relevant factors in legal and economic analyses, (2) to determine whether significantly unique results are obtained when each recognized concept of the corporation is made the basis for accounting analysis, and (3) if corporate concepts are proved to be relevant, to determine which concepts of the corporation constitute acceptable bases for the accounting analyses required to provide useful and valid information for use in the making of legal and economic decisions. Concepts: It has been found that at least four fundamental notions of the corporation have been defined and utilized in legal analysis. These are the concept of the corporation as an association of individuals, the concept of the corporation as a legal entity which is separate and distinct from those having a financial interest in it, "corporation" as merely denoting a particular set of legal relations, and the concept of the corporation as an economic entity. Each of these concepts has been found to have support in the views of some economists with respect to the relationship of the corporation and its security holders. And, likewise, each concept has been found to be consistent with a proposed "theory" of accounting (proprietary theory, entity theory, fund theory, and enterprise theory) and, frequently, to be manifested in accounting analyses proposed for specific transactions.

Effects: By utilizing each one of the four concepts of the corporation as the basis for the accounting analysis of twenty-one specific transactions considered most likely to be affected by an underlying corporate concept, it has been possible to compare the results and isolate differences.[1]

This detailed examination has shown the information accumulated and reported in accordance with the concept of the corporation as a set of legal relations to be clearly unique. It requires an accounting for the legal effects of transactions, largely as specified by state statutes, in contrast to an accounting for the economic effects of transactions as is consistent with other concepts. In only a few instances might the legal and economic effects of the specific transactions analyzed be accounted for in identical fashion.[2]

On the other hand, relatively few differences were revealed by the comparison of the results of accounting

---

[1]The twenty-one transactions referred to are listed in order of consideration in Appendix I.

[2]Namely, the accounting for stock splitups, for the issuance of bonds, and possibly for income taxes. Under certain conditions the legal and economic effects of a few other transactions might also be identical: the issuance of capital stock at par or stated value; conversion of capital stock which was originally issued at par or stated value, provided total legal capital is not changed by the conversion; and possibly the conversion of bonds to capital stock.

analyses based on the concept of the corporation as an
association of common shareholders and the concept of the
corporation as a separate and distinct entity existing for
the benefit of all its investors irrespective of their
equity classification. The treatments accorded interest
charges and preferred dividends differ. These transactions
constitute expenses of the association of common shareholders; they are distributions of the income of the separate
entity. What constitutes gains or losses on retirement of
bonds or preferred stock from the proprietary view are merely
equity adjustments from the point of view of the separate
entity. And, whereas the amount of investment contributions
and the amount of accumulated undistributed earnings of the
continuing separate and distinct corporate entity depend
upon the particular legal entity selected for survival,
these amounts are not affected by the corporate title used
for the legal convenience or the economic advantage of the
association of common shareholders. For the remainder of
the twenty-one transactions analyzed, the results obtained
on the basis of each of these two concepts are essentially
the same. Only the terminology and underlying rationaliza-
tions are apt to be at odds.

The use of the concept of the corporation as a social
institution as a basis for accounting analysis produces a
number of results significantly different from those obtained in accordance with the proprietary or entity views.
The treatment of dividends to common shareholders as an
expense of the institution differs from their treatment as

income distributions in accordance with the proprietary
and entity concepts; donations constitute a unique source
of capital rather than an augmentation of ownership or
equities; and, in contrast to the concept of separate and
distinct entity, the accounts of the enterprise arising from
a pooling of interests are not affected by the selection of
the corporate name.

As noted earlier, the incorporated social institution
may also be thought of separately and distinctly from the
contributors of its capital. The accounts of the social
institution, however, are constructed to provide information for society in general rather than primarily for the
corporation's common shareholders or other equityholders.
Thus, by obviating consideration of the legal ramifications
of ownership and equities, the analysis consistent with the
institutional concept is comparatively straight-forward.
In particular, problems created by premium on preferred
stock and the retirement of bonds and preferred stock at
amounts greater or less than book value are eliminated.
Conclusions: The concept of the corporation as representing
merely a particular set of legal relations is not an acceptable basis for accounting analysis. There can be no question that the legal effects of transactions are important
considerations in implementing the protection of corporate
creditors and investors afforded by the provisions of state
statutes. Some legal distinctions, however, are arbitrary
and artificial, e.g., the separate treatments of par values
and premiums. And there is considerable doubt, therefore,

whether the data accumulated for legal purposes is desirable
or even useful information for nonlegal decisions such as
decisions to purchase, retain, or dispose of corporate
securities.

Furthermore, the strictly legal concept of the corporation is not an acceptable basis for accounting analysis
because "corporation" does not denote a uniform set of legal
relations. As demonstrated by the comparison of the legal
effects designated in the states of California and Minnesota,
the provisions of corporation statutes of individual states
are apt to vary significantly.

The concept of the corporation as a separate and distinct legal entity existing and operating for the benefit
of all its investors is likewise deemed unacceptable as a
basis for accounting analysis. It is unsatisfactory to
attempt to rationalize the position that the interests of
bondholders, preferred shareholders, and common shareholders
are entirely compatible. This may be illustrated by the
anomally of viewing the payment of interest as the distribution of entity income in the absence of corporate earnings,
either current or accumulated. It is similarly difficult
to rationalize the retirement of bonds or preferred stock
at an amount less than book value as constituting merely
an equity adjustment of mutual advantage or mutual indiffer-
ence to the equityholders affected. But it is particularly
unsatisfactory to rely upon a corporate concept which calls
for different sets of accounting information in the face of
identical economic facts--specifically, which calls for

different amounts of investment contributions and accumulated undistributed earnings, depending upon the expedient choice of a corporate name, in the case of a pooling of interests.

As noted above, the results obtained from accounting analyses based on the association of individuals concept and on the concept of separate and distinct entity are largely the same. Where they differ, the analysis in accordance with the association view is more defensible. In the examination of the effects of the twenty-one transactions, no irrational or inexplicable results were obtained by basing the analysis on the corporation as an association of common shareholders. Further, it is to be noted in favor of this concept, that when the popular legal concept of separate and distinct entity proves to be inconvenient in the administration of justice, the courts have found it necessary to admit that fundamentally the corporation must be recognized as an association of individuals.[1]

The important question that arises, however, is whether the proprietary view is realistic in the case of the large corporation whose securities are widely distributed. Certainly, the notion of proprietorship has little meaning in the case of a corporation such as the American Telephone and Telegraph Company, particularly when the dollar terms in which it is measured have no validity.

The concept of the corporation as a social institution has been proposed for the large, publicly-held

---

[1] See p. 16, supra.

corporation. Although it has been suggested that this concept is restricted to corporations whose common stocks are
listed on a national or regional stock exchange--a convenient
and well-defined distinction--it would seem that the essence
of this institutional concept might be extended to corporations whose securities, though unlisted, are, nevertheless,
publicly held. Indeed, the essence of the institutional
concept might well be applicable to all corporations.

Treatment of the corporation as a unique economic
institution embraces the most desirable aspect of the "entity
theory" of accounting, namely, the separateness and distinct-
ness of the corporate entity, and rejects the "entity
theory's" undesirable aspects, i.e., the concern with the
notion of equities and the pre-eminence of the artificial
legal entity. Thus, preoccupation with quantifying the
interests of a particular group of investors may be eliminated and the basic economic effects of transactions are
made paramount.

Whether the corporation be regarded as an institution
intended for economic growth and development in the interests
of society in general, be regarded as an institution existing and operating for the benefit of all those who have
contributed to its capital, or be regarded as an institution existing and operating primarily for the benefit of
those investors bearing the greatest risk and possessing
ultimate decision-making power, the information accumulated
and reported as a result of the accounting process consistent with the concept of the corporation as an economic

institution holds the greatest promise for general usefulness, uniformity, and acceptability.

209

APPENDIX I

1. Issuance of capital stock--common
2. Issuance of capital stock--preferred
3. Purchase of treasury stock
4. Retirement of treasury stock
5. Reissuance of treasury stock
6. Stock dividends
7. Stock splitups
8. Conversion of capital stock
9. Issuance of bonds
10. Retirement of bonds at an amount less than book value
11. Retirement of bonds at an amount greater than book value
12. Conversion of bonds to capital stock
13. Interest charges
14. Income taxes
15. Dividends
16. Donations of outstanding shares
17. Gratuitous forgiveness of obligations
18. Donations of assets
19. Appreciation
20. Appropriations of accumulated undistributed earnings
21. Business combinations

BIBLIOGRAPHY

Books

Accounting

American Institute of Accountants. Accounting Trends and Techniques in Published Corporate Annual Reports. 8th ed. New York: American Institute of Accountants, 1954.

Canning, John B. The Economics of Accountancy. New York: The Ronald Press Company, 1929.

Finney, H. A., and Miller, Herbert E. Principles of Accounting, Advanced. 4th ed. New York: Prentice-Hall, Inc., 1952.

_____. Principles of Accounting, Intermediate. 4th ed. New York: Prentice-Hall, Inc., 1951.

Gilman, Stephen. Accounting Concepts of Profit. New York: The Ronald Press Company, 1939.

Hatfield, Henry Rand. Surplus and Dividends. Cambridge: Harvard University Press, 1947.

Karrenbrock, Wilbert E., and Simons, Harry. Intermediate Accounting. Standard vol., 2d ed. Cincinnati: South-Western Publishing Company, 1954.

Kester, Roy B. Principles of Accounting. 4th ed. New York: The Ronald Press Company, 1939.

Kohler, Eric L. A Dictionary for Accountants. New York: Prentice-Hall, Inc., 1952.

Littleton, A. C. Accounting Evolution to 1900. New York: American Institute Publishing Co., Inc., 1933.

Marple, Raymond Parker. Capital Surplus and Corporate Net Worth. New York: The Ronald Press Company, 1936.

Mason, Perry, and Davidson, Sidney. Fundamentals of Accounting. 3d ed. Brooklyn: The Foundation Press, Inc., 1953.

Moonitz, Maurice. The Entity Theory of Consolidated Statements. Brooklyn: The Foundation Press, Inc., 1951.

211

Moonitz, Maurice, and Staehling, Charles C. Accounting,
An Analysis of Its Problems. 2 vols. Brooklyn: The
Foundation Press, Inc., 1952.

Newlove, George Hillis, and Garner, S. Paul. Advanced
Accounting. Vol. I. Boston: D. C. Heath and Company,
1951.

Paton, William A. (ed.). Accountants' Handbook. 3d ed.
New York: The Ronald Press Company, 1948.

_____. Accounting Theory. New York: The Ronald Press
Company, 1922.

_____. Essentials of Accounting. New York: The Macmillan
Company, 1938.

_____. Essentials of Accounting. Revised ed. New York:
The Macmillan Company, 1949.

_____ and Littleton, A. C. An Introduction to Corporate
Accounting Standards. American Accounting Association,
1940.

_____ and Paton, William A., Jr. Corporation Accounts and
Statements. New York: The Macmillan Company, 1955.

Simpson, Kemper. Economics for the Accountant. New York,
London: D. Appleton and Company, 1921.

Sprague, Charles E. The Philosophy of Accounts. New York:
The Ronald Press Company, 1922.

Sunley, William T., and Carter, William J. Corporation
Accounting. Revised ed. New York: The Ronald Press
Company, 1944.

United States Securities and Exchange Commission. Accounting
Series Releases. Washington, D. C.: United States
Government Printing Office, 1948.

Vatter, William J. "Corporate Stock Equities," Handbook
of Modern Accounting Theory. Edited by Morton Backer.
New York: Prentice-Hall, Inc., 1955.

_____. The Fund Theory of Accounting and Its Implications
for Financial Reports. Chicago: The University of
Chicago Press, 1947.

Economics and Finance

Barnett, George E., "The Entrepreneur and the Supply of
Capital," Economic Essays Contributed in Honor of John
Bates Clark. Edited by Jacob H. Hollander. New York:
The Macmillan Company, 1927.

212

Beckerath, Herbert von. Modern Industrial Organization. New York and London: McGraw-Hill Book Company, Inc., 1933.

Berle, A. A., Jr., and Means, Gardiner C. "Corporation," Encyclopaedia of the Social Sciences. Vol. IV. New York: The Macmillan Company, 1931.

_____. The Modern Corporation and Private Property. New York: The Macmillan Company, 1936.

Boulding, Kenneth E. Economic Analysis. Revised ed. New York: Harper & Brothers Publishers, 1948.

Bowman, Mary Jean, and Bach, George Leland. Economic Analysis and Public Policy. 2d ed. New York: Prentice-Hall, Inc., 1950.

Brownlee, O. H., and Edward D. Allen. Economics of Public Finance. 2d ed. New York: Prentice-Hall, Inc., 1954.

Buchanan, Norman S. The Economics of Corporate Enterprise. New York: Henry Holt and Company, 1940.

Clark, John Bates. Essentials of Economic Theory. New York: The Macmillan Company, 1918.

Dewing, Arthur Stone. The Financial Policy of Corporations. Vol. I, 5th ed. New York: The Ronald Press Company, 1953.

_____. A Study of Corporation Securities. New York: The Ronald Press Company, 1934.

Dobb, Maurice. "Entrepreneur," Encyclopaedia of the Social Sciences. Vol. V. New York: The Macmillan Company, 1931.

Fisher, Irving. The Nature of Capital and Income. New York: The Macmillan Company, 1906.

Gordon, Robert A. "Enterprise Profits and the Modern Corporation," Explorations in Economics: Notes and Essays Contributed in Honor of F. W. Taussig. New York and London, McGraw-Hill Book Company, Inc., 1936.

Groves, Harold M. Financing Government. 4th ed. New York: Henry Holt and Company, 1954.

Guthmann, Harry G., and Dougall, Herbert E. Corporate Financial Policy. 3d ed. New York: Prentice-Hall, Inc., 1955.

Hardy, Charles O. Risk and Risk-Bearing. Revised ed. Chicago: The University of Chicago Press, 1931.

Harvard University, Research Center in Entrepreneurial
History. Change and the Entrepreneur: Postulates
and Patterns for Entrepreneurial History. Cambridge:
Harvard University Press, 1949.

Hicks, J. R. Value and Capital. 2d ed. London: Oxford
University Press, 1950.

Knight, Frank H. Risk, Uncertainty, and Profit. Boston
and New York: Houghton Mifflin Company, 1921.

Owens, Richard Norman. Business Organization and Combination.
New York: Prentice-Hall, Inc., 1951.

Ripley, William Z. Main Street and Wall Street. Boston:
Little, Brown, and Company, 1927.

Schumpeter, Joseph A. "Economic Theory and Entrepreneurial
History," Essays of J. A. Schumpeter. Edited by Richard
V. Clemence. Cambridge: Addison-Wesley Press, Inc.,
1951.

Seager, Henry Rogers, and Gulick, Charles A., Jr. Trust
and Corporation Problems. New York and London: Harper &
Brothers Publishers, 1929.

Taylor, F. M. Principles of Economics. 8th ed. New York:
The Ronald Press Company, 1923.

Tuttle, Charles A. "A Functional Theory of Economic Profit,"
Economic Essays Contributed in Honor of John Bates Clark.
Edited by Jacob H. Hollander. New York: The Macmillan
Company, 1927.

Wormser, I. Maurice. Frankenstein, Incorporated. New
York: McGraw-Hill Book Company, Inc., 1931.

Law

Anderson, Walter Houston. Limitations of the Corporate
Entity. St. Louis, Thomas Law Book Company, 1931.

Angell, Joseph K., and Ames, Samuel. Treatise on the Law
of Private Corporations Aggregate. 11th ed. Revised,
corrected, and enlarged by John Lathrop. Boston:
Little, Brown, and Company, 1882.

Blackstone, William. Commentaries on the Laws of England.
Vol. I, 7th ed. Oxford: Clarendon Press, 1775.

Carter, James Treat. The Nature of the Corporation as a
Legal Entity. Baltimore: M. Curlander, 1919.

Coke, Edward. The First Part of the Institutes of the
Lawes of England or A Commentarie upon Littleton, not
the name of a Lawyer onely, but of the Law it selfe.
London: Printed for the Societe of Stationers, 1628.

Cook, William W. A Treatise on the Law of Corporations
Having a Capital Stock. Vol. I, 8th ed. New York:
Baker, Voorhis & Co., 1923.

Dewey, John. Philosophy and Civilization. New York:
Minton, Palch & Company, 1931.

Fletcher, William Meade. Cyclopedia of the Law of Private
Corporations. Vol. I. Revised and Permanent ed.
Chicago: Callaghan and Company, 1931.

Freund, Ernst. The Legal Nature of Corporations. Chicago:
The University of Chicago Press, 1897.

Gierke, Otto Friedrich von. Political Theories of the
Middle Age. Translated with an introduction by Frederic
William Maitland. Cambridge: University Press, 1900.

Gray, John Chipman. The Nature and Sources of the Law.
2d ed. New York: The Macmillan Company, 1927.

Hallis, Frederick. Corporate Personality: A Study in
Jurisprudence. London: Oxford University Press, 1930.

Henderson, Gerard Carl. The Position of Foreign Corporations
in American Constitutional Law. Cambridge: Harvard
University Press, 1918.

Hohfeld, Wesley Newcomb. Fundamental Legal Conceptions as
Applied in Judicial Reasoning and Other Legal Essays.
New Haven: Yale University Press, 1923.

Kent, James. Commentaries on American Law. Vol. II, 14th
ed. Edited by John M. Gould. Boston: Little, Brown,
and Company, 1896.

Kyd, Stewart. A Treatise on the Law of Corporations.
London: J. Butterworth, Fleet-Street, 1793.

Latty, Elvin R. Subsidiaries and Affiliated Corporations.
Chicago: The Foundation Press, Inc., 1936.

Morawetz, Victor. A Treatise on the Law of Private Corporations. Vol. I, 2d ed. Boston: Little, Brown,
and Company, 1886.

Stevens, Robert S. Handbook on the Law of Private Corporations. St. Paul: West Publishing Co., 1936.

_____. Handbook on the Law of Private Corporations.
2d ed. St. Paul: West Publishing Co., 1949.

Taylor, Henry Osborn. A Treatise on the Law of Private
    Corporations. 5th ed. New York: The Banks Law
    Publishing Co., 1905.

Thompson, Seymour D., and Thompson, Joseph W. Commentaries
    on the Law of Corporations. Vol. I, 3d ed.
    Indianapolis: The Bobbs-Merrill Company, 1927.

Wormser, I. Maurice. Disregard of the Corporate Fiction
    and Allied Corporation Problems. New York: Baker,
    Voorhis and Company, 1927.

                            Articles

Accounting

Bangs, Robert B. "The Definition and Measurement of
    Income," The Accounting Review, XV (September, 1940),
    353-371.

Black, W. M. "Certain Phases of Merger Accounting," The
    Journal of Accountancy, LXXXIII (March, 1947), 214-220.

Blough, Carman G. "Summary of Facts and Comments Concerning
    a Recent Merger," The Journal of Accountancy, LXXXVIII
    (July, 1949), 82-84.

Borth, Daniel. "Donated Fixed Assets," The Accounting
    Review, XXIII (April, 1948), 171-178.

Bowers, Russell. "Some Unsettled Problems of Income,"
    The Accounting Review, XV (September, 1940), 350-353.

Chow, Y. C. "The Concept of Expense," The Accounting Review,
    XIV (December, 1939), 340-349.

_____. "The Doctrine of Proprietorship," The Accounting
    Review, XVII (April, 1942), 157-163.

Dohr, James L. "Capital and Surplus in the Corporate
    Balance Sheet," The Accounting Review, XIV (March, 1939),
    38-42.

Husband, George R. "The Corporate-Entity Fiction and
    Accounting Theory," The Accounting Review, XIII
    (September, 1938), 241-253.

_____. "The Entity Concept in Accounting," The Accounting
    Review, XXIX (October, 1954), 552-563.

Lund, Reuel I. "Realizable Value As a Measurement of Gross
    Income," The Accounting Review, XVI (December, 1941),
    373-385.

Marvin, J. Arthur. "Corporate Consolidations, Reorganizations and Mergers," The New York Certified Public Accountant, XV (July, 1945), 366-373

Paton, William A. "Is It Desirable to Distinguish between Various Kinds of Surplus?--A Symposium," The Journal of Accountancy, LXV (April, 1938), 281-292.

Seidman, Nelson B. "The Determination of Stockholder Income," The Accounting Review, XXXI (January, 1956), 64-70.

Simon, Sidney I. "Legal Decisions on the Accounting for Corporate Surplus," The Accounting Review, XXXI (January, 1956), 104-108.

Stevens, W. H. S. "Stockholders' Participations in Assets in Dissolution," The Journal of Business of the University of Chicago, X (January, 1937), 46-73.

Suojanen, Waino W. "Accounting Theory and the Large Corporation," The Accounting Review, XXIX (July, 1954), 391-398.

Werntz, William W. "Corporate Consolidations, Reorganizations and Mergers," The New York Certified Public Accountant, XV (July, 1945), 379-387.

Wilcox, Edward B. "Accounting for Stock Dividends: A Dissent from Current Recommended Practice," The Journal of Accountancy, XCVI (August, 1953), 176-181.

_____. "Business Combinations: An Analysis of Mergers, Purchases, and Related Accounting Procedure," The Journal of Accountancy, LXXXIX (February, 1950), 102-107.

Economics and Finance

Berle, A. A., Jr., and Means, Gardiner C. "Corporations and the Public Investor," The American Economic Review, XX (March, 1930), 54-71.

Churchill, Betty C. "Business Population by Legal Form of Organization," Survey of Current Business, XXXV (April, 1955).

Coase, R. H. "The Nature of the Firm," Economica, VI (August, 1937), 386-405.

Fergusson, Donald A. "Recent Developments in Preferred Stock Financing," The Journal of Finance, VII (September, 1952), 447-462.

217

Gordon, Robert A. "Stockholdings of Officers and Directors in American Industrial Corporations," Quarterly Journal of Economics, L (August, 1936), 622-657.

Hart, Albert G. "Anticipations, Planning, and the Business Cycle," Quarterly Journal of Economics, LI (February, 1937), 273-297.

Kaldor, Nicholas. "The Equilibrium of the Firm," Economic Journal, XLIV (March, 1934), 60-76.

Knauth, Oswald W. "Group Interest and Managerial Enterprise," Journal of Industrial Economics, I (April, 1953), 88-98.

Lewis, Ben W. "The Corporate Entrepreneur," The Quarterly Journal of Economics, LI (May, 1937), 535-544.

Means, Gardiner C. "The Large Corporation in American Economic Life," The American Economic Review, XXI (March, 1931), 10-42.

Soule, Roland P. "Trends in the Cost of Capital," Harvard Business Review, XXXI (March-April, 1953), 33-47.

Stauss, James H. "The Entrepreneur: The Firm," Journal of Political Economy, LII (June, 1944), 112-127.

Taussig, F. W., and Barker, W. S. "American Corporations and Their Executives: A Statistical Inquiry," Quarterly Journal of Economics, XL (November, 1925), 1-51.

Tuttle, Charles A. "The Entrepreneur Function in Economic Literature," Journal of Political Economy, XXXV (August, 1927), 501-521.

_____. "The Function of the Entrepreneur," American Economic Review, XVII (March, 1927), 13-25.

Law

Anonymous. "'Corporate Entity'--Its Limitations as a Useful Legal Conception," Yale Law Journal, XXXVI (December, 1926), 254-260.

_____. "Evolution of the Corporate Entity," Corporate Practice Review, III (November, 1931), 63-68.

_____. "The Legal Idea of a Corporation," The American Law Review, XIX (January-February, 1885), 114-116.

Berle, Adolf A., Jr. "The Theory of Enterprise Entity," Columbia Law Review, XLVII (April, 1947), 343-358.

Brown, W. Jethro. "The Personality of the Corporation and the State," The Law Quarterly Review, XXI (October, 1905), 365-379.

Canfield, George F. "The Scope and Limits of the Corporate Entity Theory," Columbia Law Review, XVII (February, 1917), 128-143.

Dix, Maurice J. "The Economic Entity," Fordham Law Review, XXII (December, 1953), 254-273.

Geldart, W. M. "Legal Personality," The Law Quarterly Review, XXVII (January, 1911), 90-108.

Israel, Abner M. "The Legal Fiction of Corporate Entity and Modern Law," Georgia Bar Journal, III (August, 1940), 46-56.

Kessel, Lawrence P. "Trends in the Approach to the Corporate Entity Problem in Civil Litigation," The Georgetown Law Journal, XLI (May, 1953), 525-542.

Laski, Harold J. "The Personality of Associations," Harvard Law Review, XXIX (February, 1916), 404-426.

Lyon, Hastings. "What Is a Corporation?" Corporate Practice Review, I (May, 1929), 7-15.

Machen, Arthur W., Jr. "Corporate Personality," Harvard Law Review, XXIV (February and March, 1911), 253-267, 347-365.

Pinney, Harvey. "The Nature of the Corporation," Temple University Law Quarterly, XIV (July, 1940), 443-473.

Pollock, Frederick. "Has the Common Law Received the Fiction Theory of Corporations?" The Law Quarterly Review, XXVII (April, 1911), 219-235.

Radin, Max. "The Endless Problem of Corporate Personality," Columbia Law Review, XXXII (April, 1932), 643-667.

Raymond, Robert L. "The Genesis of the Corporation," Harvard Law Review, XIX (March, 1906), 350-365.

Saxon, Sidney. "Is the Problem of Disregarding the Corporate Entity More A Question of Fact than of Law?" St. John's Law Review, XI (April, 1937), 294-302.

Sharratt, George S. H., Jr. "Corporations--Nature and Theory--Why Corporate Entity?" Missouri Law Review, I (June, 1936), 278-281.

Smith, Bryant. "Legal Personality," Yale Law Journal, XXXVII (January, 1928), 283-299.

Williams, Henry Winslow. "An Inquiry Into the Nature
and Law of Corporations," The American Law Register,
XLVII(OS) (January, February, and March, 1899), 1-16,
65-77, and 137-150.

Wise, Joseph. "Due Process: Corporation As An Economic
Unit," University of Cincinnati Law Review, XIII
(May, 1939), 460-468.

Professional Accounting Society Reports

American Institute of Accountants, Committee on Accounting
Procedure. "Corporate Accounting for Ordinary Stock
Dividends," Accounting Research Bulletins, No. 11
(September, 1941).

_____. "Depreciation on Appreciation," Accounting Research
Bulletins, No. 5 (April, 1940).

_____. "Report of Committee on Terminology," Accounting
Research Bulletins, No. 9 (Special) (May, 1941).

_____. "Restatement and Revision of Accounting Research
Bulletins," Accounting Research Bulletin, No. 43 (1953).

_____, Committee on Terminology. "Proceeds, Revenue,
Income, Profit, and Earnings," Accounting Terminology
Bulletins, No. 2(March, 1955).

_____. "Review and Resume," Accounting Terminology
Bulletins, No. 1 (1953).

American Accounting Association, Committee on Concepts
and Standards Underlying Corporate Financial Statements. "Standards of Disclosure for Published
Financial Reports," Supplementary Statement No. 8,
The Accounting Review, XXX (July, 1953), 400-404.

_____, Executive Committee. Accounting Concepts and
Standards Underlying Corporate Financial Statements
(1948 Revision).

Legal Decisions

Baltimore & Potomac Railroad Company v. Fifth Baptist
Church, 108 U.S. 317 (1883).

Berry v. Old South Engraving Co., 186 N.E. 601 (1933).

The Cincinnati Volksblatt Company v. Hoffmeister,
62 Ohio 189 (1900)

Clarke v. Bennett et al., 284 N.W. 876 (1939).

Continental Tyre & Rubber Co., Ltd. v. Daimler Co.,
    1 K.B. 893 (1915)

Department of Banking v. Hedges et al., 286 N.W. 277 (1939).

Farmers' Loan & Trust Co. v. Pierson et al., 222 N.Y.S. 532
    (1927).

Hale v. Henkel, 201 U.S. 43 (1906).

Kavanaugh v. Kavanaugh Knitting Co., Inc. et al.,
    123 Northeastern Reporter 148.

Marshall v. Baltimore and Ohio Railroad Company,
    16 Howard 314 (1853).

Matthews et al. v. Minnesota Tribune Co., 10 N.W.(2d) 230
    (1943).

Metropolitan Holding Company v. Snyder, 79 Fed(2d) 263
    (1935).

People's Pleasure Park Co., Inc. et al. v. Rohleder,
    61 S.E. 794 (1908).

In re Pittsburgh Rys. Co., 155 Fed(2d) 477 (1946).

State, ex rel. v. Standard Oil Company, 49 Ohio 137 (1892).

In re Steinberg's Estate, 274 N.Y.S. 914 (1934).

The Case of Sutton's Hospital, 10 Coke 1.

The Trustees of Dartmouth College v. Woodward,
    4 Wheaton 519 (1819).

United States v. Lehigh Valley Railroad Company,
    220 U.S. 257 (1911).

United States v. Milwaukee Refrigerator Transit Co. et al.,
    142 Fed 247 (1905).

United States v. Trinidad Coal and Coking Company,
    137 U.S. 160 (1890).

Wood v. Guarantee Trust and Safe Deposit Company,
    128 U.S. 416 (1888).